RAMSAY IN 10

GORDON RAMSAY
RAMSAY IN 10

Delicious Recipes Made in a Flash

Photography by Jamie Orlando Smith

GRAND CENTRAL
PUBLISHING

NEW YORK BOSTON

CONTENTS

Introduction

When I wrote my previous book, *Quick and Delicious*, I set myself the challenge of cooking impressive meals in 30 minutes, and it really was a challenge. I had to rethink the ingredients I could use, look at which techniques would be quick enough, and find new ways to inject flavour in a short space of time. But sometimes a constraint can drive creativity in the kitchen, and I loved the results. Little did I know that the time frame was about to get even shorter!

Ramsay in 10 started as a fun idea for my YouTube channel. The plan was to see whether my fellow chefs could cook classic dishes in just ten minutes, but then, in March 2020, the world went into lockdown, and instead of sending a camera crew round to Gino D'Acampo's house, I ended up challenging myself while staying at home in Cornwall in the UK. My daughters were in charge of lighting and filming, and the dishes were our family favourites, all made with the ingredients we could get hold of locally. It was fast-paced and fun, and it got me thinking about what can be achieved in a ten-minute time frame. I now believe that, armed with the right knowledge and a few clever short cuts, it's absolutely possible to cook amazing food from scratch in very little time. This collection of 100 great recipes is testament to that.

But speed in the kitchen is an individual thing – everybody moves at a different pace. After years of training and experience, professional chefs like me can obviously cook faster and more confidently than most people at home. What I'm trying to say is that while I might be able to cook these dishes in ten minutes, you might take a little bit longer until you know the recipe well and can anticipate what's coming up next. But who's timing you? Trust me, I'm not going to come round with a stopwatch and start swearing at you if you go over by a minute or two!

Generally, if you aim for ten minutes, you are likely to have food on the table in 15 to 20, but if you pick a 30-minute recipe, it's likely to take you around 40 to 45, especially if it's the first time you have tackled it. So while this is definitely fast food, and before you take to social media to protest otherwise, you might not always get everything finished in the ten-minute time frame. In part, that's because I haven't compromised on the standard of each dish and have tried to pack in as much flavour as possible. And also, ten minutes is a really short amount of time. Even I sometimes struggled to keep to the time limit – I mostly blame my daughters' heckling for that – but I had fun trying and, more importantly, ate some great food.

In this book, I've tried to condense all of my experience and knowledge into a collection of recipes that deliver on both the taste and timing fronts. I hope it inspires you to get into the kitchen, knowing that great food is only a matter of minutes away. In fact, what are you waiting for?

Chop chop...

Gordon x

 YouTube Gordon Ramsay   @gordongram   @GordonRamsay   Gordon Ramsay

What to expect from this book...

FAST FOOD

This book offers fast food at its finest, and fine food at its fastest! Maybe not quicker than a ready meal in a microwave, but definitely faster than a takeaway delivery. The recipes have been developed to take around ten minutes, with an absolute maximum of ten minutes prep and ten minutes cooking (apart from the Rhubarb and Marzipan Tarts (see page 234), which take a bit longer to cook). However, the point isn't just to help you to cook faster, but to inspire you to get into the kitchen to cook from scratch more often. I'm hoping that the guarantee of a quick turnaround will do exactly that.

GREAT FOOD

This isn't just fast food, this is really tasty, satisfying food that happens to be quick to put together. I've borrowed ideas and flavours from different cuisines around the world, and really packed a lot into the ten-minute time frame. It takes less than ten minutes to whip up a plain omelette, but wouldn't you rather a Mozzarella and Basil Omelette with Asparagus and Shiitake Mushrooms (see page 20)? Expect to try new ingredients, unexpected combinations and some sped-up versions of old favourites.

CLEVER SHORT CUTS

As you can imagine, working in a fast-paced, highly pressurised restaurant kitchen for so many years has taught me a thing or two about cutting corners in cooking without compromising on results. In this book, I'm sharing some of that know-how to help you cook more efficiently and effectively at home. These are tricks and tips that you can use every day to make producing great food easier and quicker.

HONESTY

The last thing I want to hear of is you throwing this book across the room in frustration because you feel I haven't kept to my side of the bargain... As I've said, ten minutes is tight, and some of these recipes will be more challenging to get done on time than others. Where I think the recipe will definitely take you a bit longer than ten minutes, I warn you in the introduction. I've also admitted when I've gone over the time limit myself – not least because the evidence is on YouTube for everyone to see!

OPTIONS

As the recipe time is so short, I've made some elements of the dishes optional. For example, you can choose whether to garnish a pasta dish with a few chopped herbs or make a crispy breadcrumb pangritata to sprinkle over the top. I've also made some serving suggestions that will add to your overall time if you choose to include them, and there are plenty of alternatives given for when you can't get hold of an ingredient or you just fancy a change. You're in charge here, but I like to think that I have given you plenty to work with, as well as lots of tasty incentives for going the extra mile.

KEY TO SYMBOLS:

V   Vegetarian

VG   Vegan

GF   Gluten-free

DF   Dairy-free

Scan this QR Code to Watch Ramsay in 10 on YouTube.

What this book expects from you...

If you want to cook good food fast, there are a few rules. This might sound bossy (who, me?), but I want to make it easier for you to get great results in a short amount of time. If you follow these instructions, I guarantee you will be quicker and better in the kitchen.

TO BUY GOOD INGREDIENTS
When cooking at speed, every ingredient matters. The better the produce, the less hard you will have to work to make it taste great. Try to buy the freshest fish, the most flavourful meat and the ripest fruit and vegetables in season and you will be more than halfway there before you even start cooking.

TO GET HELP
Not with the cooking, but with the ingredients. Get your butcher to spatchcock the chicken and your fishmonger to butterfly the trout. These professionals will take seconds to do something that will take you much longer. And take advantage of all the shortcuts offered by supermarkets these days – chopped vegetables, grated cheese, ready-cooked pulses, etc. They are a godsend when time is tight.

TO READ THE RECIPE BEFORE YOU START
This will be the most valuable minute you spend. Knowing what to expect from a recipe will really help you to execute it more smoothly, and you won't be slowed down by unexpected instructions.

TO PREHEAT THE OVEN/GRILL/GRIDDLE PAN
Most ovens take about 15 minutes to get to temperature, but can differ wildly. Ten-minute cooking only works if the oven, grill (broiler) and griddle (grill) pan are ready to go when you are, so switch the heat on first.

TO GET ORGANISED
Ninety per cent of this is preparation. Once you have read through the recipe and turned the oven on, it's time to assemble and weigh out the ingredients. I have tried to put as much of the prep into the method as possible so that you make the dressing while the meat is cooking, for example, but in some cases that couldn't be done. Therefore, look out for prep instructions in the ingredients list because they need to be tackled before you start. Being organised will make the cooking a doddle.

TO HAVE THE RIGHT KIT
Throughout this book, I've tried to avoid using specialist equipment, but the following five items will definitely be useful over and over again, and will help you keep to the time limit:

- *a large rectangular griddle (grill) pan*
- *a Japanese mandoline for slicing*
- *a small, powerful food processor, such as a Nutribullet*
- *a microplane*
- *a speed peeler*

TO KEEP YOUR KNIVES SHARP
The old saying tells us 'A workman is only as good as his tools', and a sharp knife is obviously more efficient than a blunt one. It's also less dangerous because it requires less pressure and is less likely to slip. You should sharpen your knives with a steel at least once a week, depending on how often you use them.

TO FOCUS ON THE MATTER AT HAND
If you watch any of my ten-minute challenges on YouTube, you will see that I am 100 per cent focused on the cooking. Okay, not quite 100 per cent – there are plenty of interruptions by Oscar, Tana and the girls – but my point is that I'm not checking my phone, the TV isn't on in the background, and I'm not listening to the radio... Cooking at speed is fast-paced, and getting rid of distractions will help you to concentrate.

TO FOLLOW THE INSTRUCTIONS
I've written these recipes with maximum efficiency in mind at all times, so follow the instructions! Feel free to make ingredient substitutions and increase the quantities, but if you want the dish to turn out perfectly, go through the method one step at a time until you know the recipe well enough to make your own modifications.

TO GET BETTER AND BETTER WITH PRACTICE
The first time you cook a recipe, everything is unfamiliar and will take longer – just finding your place on the page and checking the instructions repeatedly will slow you down significantly. But each time you cook a dish, the less you have to check and the more confidently you can go from one step to the next. Before long you will nail it in ten minutes every time.

Quick-fix flavours

If you don't have time to let flavours develop slowly during cooking, it is very useful to have a cupboard and fridge full of pastes, sauces and spice mixes that can inject complexity and interest into your food in an instant. Here is a list of some of the quick-fix ingredients from this book that you might not be very familiar with.

CHIPOTLE CHILLI PASTE
Chipotle chillies are actually jalapeños that have been allowed to ripen fully on the plant, then wood-smoked to give them a sweet smokiness while retaining a mild to medium heat. Used a lot in Mexican and Tex-Mex food, this versatile paste also works in dressings, marinades, soups and even chocolate sauce (see page 240).

DUKKAH
Dukkah is a Middle Eastern mixture of spices (usually cumin and coriander), sesame seeds and ground hazelnuts that is often served with bread and oil as a dip, but can also be used to inject flavour and crunch to vegetables and salads.

FURIKAKE SEASONING
This Japanese seasoning is made from toasted sesame seeds, seaweed, sugar, salt and dried shrimps (vegan versions are also available), and it's used to add a hit of salty umami to whatever it's sprinkled over. In Japan, this is usually rice, but it works well with fish, tofu and vegetables too.

GENTLEMAN'S RELISH
This punchy anchovy paste is as old-fashioned as it sounds. It has been made in England since 1828 and is delicious spread on toast or stirred into sauces and dressings for an intense salty hit.

GOCHUJANG CHILLI PASTE
Unique among chilli pastes and sauces, gochujang is fermented, which gives it a distinct pungent flavour and manages to be sweet, savoury and very hot all at the same time. It is a cornerstone of Korean cooking, and can be stirred into sauces, stews and marinades.

HARISSA
An aromatic chilli paste from North Africa, which adds instant depth and heat. The ingredients vary from country to country, and even region to region, but it is always hot, earthy and fragrant, especially if you buy rose harissa, which is made with dried rose petals.

KECAP MANIS
This Indonesian soy sauce is sweetened with palm sugar, which means it's thick and treacly but still salty. It's used in all the most famous of Indonesia's dishes, such as nasi goreng, mie goreng and gado gado (see page 198).

MIRIN
Mirin is a Japanese rice wine something like sake, but sweeter and less alcoholic. It is usually paired with soy sauce to give that distinct sweet and salty tang to Japanese sauces, broths and marinades like teriyaki.

NDUJA
Nduja is a very fiery spreadable salami from the Calabria region of southern Italy, where they serve it with bread and cheese. It can be bought in thick tranches, or in smaller quantities in jars, and is amazing stirred through pasta sauces or spread on pizza.

NORI
The dried seaweed used to wrap rice for sushi can also be used as a garnish or vegetable in its own right. It brings a satisfying hit of briny umami and plenty of nutrients to rice, ramen and other noodle dishes.

POMEGRANATE MOLASSES
Sticky pomegranate molasses is made by reducing pomegranate juice down to a thick, tangy syrup, which gives a mildly sweet but mostly sharp fruitiness to dressings, sauces and marinades.

PORCINI POWDER
Made by grinding dried porcini mushrooms to a powder, a sprinkle of this will boost the umami levels of both meaty and vegetarian dishes, giving them depth and richness in an instant.

RAS-EL-HANOUT

While there isn't one set recipe for this North African spice mix, which can contain up to 50 different ingredients, most people agree that it must include cumin, cinnamon, coriander, cardamom, ginger, cloves and allspice. It's a heady mix that instantly adds a Moroccan flavour to rubs, marinades and tagines.

SHICHIMI TOGARASHI

Also known as Japanese seven spice, this is similar to furikake seasoning, but with the added kick of Japanese pepper and chilli flakes. Use it to season rice, noodles and tofu dishes.

SICHUAN PEPPER

Sichuan peppercorns are prized not just for their flavour and heat, but also for the unique tingling effect they have on your mouth and tongue.

SRIRACHA SAUCE

Sriracha is a chilli sauce from Thailand, where it is used mainly as a dipping sauce. It is hot, obviously, but also sweet and tart, with a hint of garlic, making it a well-balanced hot sauce that is full of flavour and heat.

SUMAC

A ground spice made from dried berries, sumac has a lemon-lime tang that instantly lifts whatever it is sprinkled over. In some Middle Eastern countries, it is always on the table with salt and pepper, which shows how versatile it is, but I like it sprinkled over salads, couscous, meat and fish.

TAMARI

Tamari is a Japanese soy sauce that differs from its Chinese counterpart, and all of the many other Asian soy sauces, because it is a by-product of the fermentation process used to make miso paste. It is darker, richer and thicker than regular soy sauce and often gluten-free.

ZA'ATAR

This vibrant mix of dried thyme and/or oregano, sesame seeds and sumac is ubiquitous across the Middle East, where it is commonly spread on flatbreads before they are baked. It also brings a woody, citrussy lift to chicken and lamb, as well as to vegetable dishes and salads.

Short-cut ingredients

When time is tight, clever shopping can really help. There are so many labour-saving products available in supermarkets these days, but stick with simple, unadulterated ingredients that have just been chopped, cooked or frozen, avoiding anything that has been heavily processed with artificial flavours, emulsifiers and preservatives. In addition to the pastes, sauces and spice mixes mentioned on pages 12–13, the following are some of the helpful ingredients you have my permission to stock up on.

FREEZER

- Chopped chillies, onions and herbs

- Peas, spinach and sweetcorn

- Pizza dough

- Sliced bananas

FRIDGE

- Pre-chopped veg, especially those that are tricky to peel, such as butternut squash and pumpkin

- Cooked beetroot

- Bags of salad leaves

- Fresh pasta and noodles

- Fresh stock

- Ready-made pastry (puff and shortcrust)

- Grated cheese – can also be kept in the freezer

- Pancetta or bacon lardons

- Ginger paste/purée

- Garlic paste/purée

- Fresh breadcrumbs – can also be kept in the freezer

CUPBOARD

- Canned tomatoes and passata

- Canned beans and chickpeas (garbanzos)

- Pre-cooked rice

- Pre-cooked lentils and grains

- Canned fish – tuna, anchovies and sardines

- Roasted peppers and artichokes

- Chopped chillies in vinegar

- Chopped garlic in vinegar

- Crispy fried onions

- Panko breadcrumbs

- Meringues

Some general guidelines

ANIMAL WELFARE
Try to buy meat, eggs and dairy products from reputable farms that value the welfare of their livestock. It isn't just better for the animals, the produce is likely to be superior too.

BUTTER
I use unsalted butter for cooking because it's easier to control the seasoning. If you have only salted butter to hand, add less salt as you cook.

EGGS
All eggs used in the recipes are medium unless stated otherwise. Please buy free-range eggs if you can.

FISH
Choose fish from sustainable sources that have been caught or farmed using environmentally friendly methods.

HERBS
Bunches of herbs come in all shapes and sizes, but for this book, a bunch is 25g (1oz).

LEMONS
All lemons should be unwaxed if you are using the zest.

OIL
For frying, use vegetable oil or any other flavourless oil, such as sunflower, groundnut (peanut) or rapeseed (canola), that has a high smoke point. Use olive oil for sautéing, but never extra virgin olive oil. Save that for salad dressings and drizzling over the finished dish.

SPOON MEASURES
Unless stated otherwise, all spoon measures are level.

A WORD ABOUT PORTION SIZES
Many of the recipes in this book serve two people. This is because prepping for four or more takes longer and there is the issue of pan size and hob space – there are only so many pancakes you can cook at a time! Where possible I have given advice for doubling the quantities, but on the understanding that this is more than likely to take you over ten minutes. There are still plenty of recipes for four people, but feeding a crowd in ten minutes is really challenging, so I've mostly kept numbers down for this book.

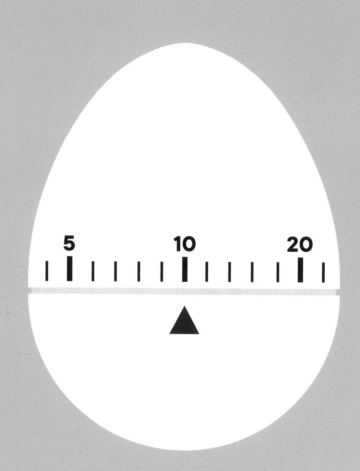

EGGS & CHEESE

Mozzarella and basil omelette with asparagus and shiitake mushrooms

A plain omelette is literally one of the fastest things you can cook – the world record is 40 seconds! But seriously, I reckon that with a bit of practice, it takes about 3 minutes from cracking the eggs to folding a finished omelette onto a plate. I've slowed things down a bit here by adding melting mozzarella to the middle, and asparagus and mushrooms to the top, but you can keep it simple by just adding some grated cheese or soft herbs.

2 tbsp olive oil

3 asparagus spears, trimmed

40g (1½oz) shiitake mushrooms

1 tbsp butter

1 garlic clove

2 tbsp white wine or water

1 tbsp crème fraîche
(sour cream)

3 eggs

60g (½ cup) mozzarella cheese,
at room temperature

Sprig of basil, leaves picked
and chopped

1 tbsp freshly grated
Parmesan cheese or
vegetarian equivalent
(optional)

1. Place a non-stick frying pan (skillet) over a medium heat and coat the bottom of the pan with 1 tablespoon of the olive oil.

2. Finely slice the asparagus spears and add them to the hot oil. Allow to cook for 2 minutes.

3. Finely slice the mushrooms and add them to the asparagus with the butter. Peel the garlic, then crush (mince) or grate it into the pan and allow to cook for 1 minute.

4. Add the wine or water and continue to cook until the liquid has reduced by half, then fold in the crème fraîche. Reduce the heat to a simmer and leave to cook until needed.

5. Crack the eggs into a bowl and whisk with a fork until combined and frothy.

6. Place a small, non-stick frying pan over a medium heat and add the remaining tablespoon of oil. When hot, pour in the eggs and allow to cook for 2 minutes, or until almost set.

7. Roughly chop the mozzarella and place it in the middle of the omelette. Fold the sides over the mozzarella, then slide the omelette onto a plate.

8. Stir the basil through the vegetable mixture and spoon it over the omelette. Finish with the grated Parmesan before serving, if using.

TIP FOR SPEED

While it is very satisfying to snap off the woody parts of asparagus one by one, using a chef's knife to cut the ends off while they are still bunched in the elastic band is much quicker.

Welsh rarebit croque-monsieurs

Here a staple British comfort food meets a French bistro classic! Basically, a posh toasted sandwich flavoured with red onion jam, Dijon mustard and Worcestershire sauce. I have used Gruyère and mozzarella, both cheeses that melt beautifully, but you can use any cheese you like, and even add a few slices of Wiltshire-cure or Bayonne ham to the sandwich, depending on which side of the Channel your preferences lie.

35g (scant ¼ cup) pancetta or streaky bacon lardons
4 thick slices of white bread, crusts removed
2½ tbsp Dijon mustard
80g (3¼oz) Gruyère cheese, sliced
2 tbsp caramelised onion jam
Dash of Worcestershire sauce
80g (⅔ cup) grated mozzarella cheese
2 tbsp red wine vinegar
2 tbsp olive oil, plus extra for frying
50g (scant ½ stick) butter
Large handful of watercress
1 head of radicchio or chicory (endive)
2 pickled onions, finely sliced
Freshly ground black pepper

1. Place a small frying pan (skillet) over a medium heat and add the pancetta or bacon lardons and a tablespoon water. Cook until bubbling, then leave to brown, stirring occasionally.

2. Meanwhile, spread two slices of the bread with the mustard, then cover with the Gruyère slices, followed by the onion jam.

3. Sprinkle a little Worcestershire sauce over the jam, then top with the grated mozzarella. Put the remaining slices of bread on top and press down to seal.

4. When the bacon is crisp, add the vinegar and 2 tablespoons oil and set aside to cool.

5. Place a large, non-stick frying pan over a medium–high heat and coat the bottom of the pan with a thin layer of oil before adding the butter.

6. When the butter begins to bubble, put the croques into the pan and allow to cook for 2–3 minutes, until golden brown. Flip them over and cook for a further 2 minutes so that both sides are brown.

7. Meanwhile, combine the watercress and radicchio leaves in a salad bowl, add the pickled onions, then pour in the bacon dressing and toss well.

8. Transfer the croques to plates and season with pepper. Serve with the salad.

Green shakshuka

Shakshuka, the North African dish of eggs baked in spicy tomato sauce, has become an essential item on brunch menus everywhere. In this version, the eggs are cooked within a bed of mixed green vegetables instead of tomatoes, making it extremely healthy, delicious and, more importantly, really quick. You can substitute my suggestions with any green vegetables you like or have knocking around in the fridge.

100ml (scant ½ cup) double (heavy) cream
60g (generous ¼ cup) cream cheese
2 tbsp chopped soft herbs, e.g. basil, chives, tarragon or parsley
Olive oil, for frying
1 banana shallot, peeled
50g (2oz) asparagus, trimmed
50g (2oz) kale
100g (⅔ cup) peas
100g (scant 1 cup) sliced courgette (zucchini)
4 eggs
Sea salt and freshly ground black pepper

To serve
3½ tbsp natural (plain) yoghurt
1 tsp chilli oil
Large handful of rocket (arugula) or watercress
1 tbsp freshly grated Parmesan cheese or vegetarian equivalent
Toasted sourdough or flatbreads

1. Whisk the cream and cream cheese together in a large bowl, then stir through the soft herbs.

2. Place a flameproof casserole dish (Dutch oven) over a medium heat and coat the bottom with a thin layer of olive oil.

3. Grate the shallot, add it to the dish and cook for 1 minute. Add the asparagus and cook for 1 minute before adding the kale, peas and courgette slices. Allow to cook for another minute. Add the cream cheese and herb mixture, season with salt and pepper and mix well.

4. Make four wells in the vegetables and crack an egg into each one. Put a lid on the dish and allow to cook for 3 minutes, until the egg whites are firm but the yolks are still runny.

5. Take the dish off the heat, then drizzle the yoghurt and chilli oil over the shakshuka. Sprinkle with the rocket or watercress and the Parmesan. Serve with toasted sourdough or warm flatbreads.

Pepper and paprika tortilla

This tortilla is inspired by a staff meal they used to make at El Bulli in Spain, once the greatest restaurant in the world, now sadly closed. Instead of making a labour-intensive and slow-to-cook tortilla with sliced potatoes, they would use crisps (potato chips), meaning it would be ready in minutes instead of hours. Sounds weird, but trust me, it's genius. You can swap the paprika crisps for plain or any other flavour if you like.

4 eggs
100g (4oz) roasted (bell) peppers, from a jar
70g (2¾oz) paprika crisps (potato chips)
40g (⅓ cup) grated mozzarella cheese
1 tbsp butter
40g (1½oz) goats' cheese
1 tsp thyme leaves, plus extra for sprinkling
Sea salt and freshly ground black pepper
Mixed leaf salad, to serve

1. Preheat the grill (broiler) to high.

2. Crack the eggs into a bowl and whisk until fully combined and frothy.

3. Chop the peppers and add them to the eggs along with the thyme leaves, crisps and mozzarella. Season with salt and pepper.

4. Place a small ovenproof frying pan (skillet) over a medium heat and add the butter. When it is foaming, pour in the egg mixture and stir with a rubber spatula for 2 minutes.

5. Once the egg is almost set, use a plate or board to flip the tortilla and continue to cook for another 2 minutes.

6. Crumble the goats' cheese over the tortilla and sprinkle with the thyme leaves.

7. Slide the tortilla onto a plate and serve with a mixed leaf salad.

Lucky Cat shrimp omelette

This omelette is from Lucky Cat, my pan-Asian restaurant in London, and was inspired by a trip to Laos for my National Geographic series, *Uncharted*. I love the combination of fish sauce, coriander (cilantro) and chilli with the brown shrimp that are native to the UK, but it works really well with regular prawns (shrimp) too. Serve with sticky rice, virtually the national dish of Laos, and a green salad.

2 tbsp fish sauce
2 tbsp lime juice
1 tbsp caster (superfine) sugar
4 eggs
1 heaped tbsp cornflour (cornstarch)
Reserved coriander (cilantro) stalks (see below)
100g (1 cup) fresh or frozen cooked and peeled brown (baby) shrimp
4 tbsp groundnut (peanut) or vegetable oil
Sea salt

To serve
Small handful of coriander (cilantro) leaves, dill and mint, coriander stalks reserved and chopped
1 tbsp crispy fried onions
½ red chilli, deseeded if you want a milder heat, finely sliced
Chilli oil, for drizzling

1. Put the fish sauce, lime juice and sugar into a bowl and add 1 tablespoon water. Season with a pinch of salt and mix well.

2. Crack the eggs into a separate bowl, then add the cornflour, coriander stalks and the fish sauce mixture. Beat together until fully combined.

3. Stir in the shrimps.

4. Place a small, non-stick frying pan (skillet) over a medium heat and add the groundnut oil. When very hot, pour in the egg mixture and allow to cook for 30–60 seconds, until puffed up and beginning to brown. Using a board or plate, flip it over and cook for a further 30 seconds.

5. Fold the omelette over and slide onto a plate. Garnish with the coriander, dill and mint leaves, the crispy onions and red chilli, and drizzle over some chilli oil.

Indian rice flour pancakes with lime pickle yoghurt

Usually, the batter for this south Indian breakfast staple needs to ferment overnight, but I've added baking powder and extra bicarbonate of soda (baking soda) so it works immediately. The colour of the finished pancakes will depend on which lentils you use – these were made with black lentils, which has turned them quite red. Lime pickle (which you can find at Asian supermarkets) yoghurt is so easy to make, and it goes beautifully with grilled fish or meat and almost any curry.

100g (⅝ cup) plain (all-purpose) flour
150g (scant 1 cup) rice flour
1 tsp baking powder
1 tsp bicarbonate of soda (baking soda)
½ tsp ground turmeric
½ tsp salt
150ml (⅔ cup) coconut or almond milk
100g (½ cup) cooked lentils
½ tsp cumin seeds
1 tsp finely chopped green chilli, deseeded if you want a milder heat
Sunflower oil, for frying

For the lime pickle yoghurt
2 tbsp smooth lime pickle
6 tbsp natural (plain) yoghurt

To serve
1 tbsp coriander (cilantro) leaves
Lime wedges

1. Put both the flours into a blender with the baking powder, bicarbonate of soda, turmeric, salt, coconut milk and 100ml (scant ½ cup) water and blend until smooth.

2. Fold in the lentils, cumin seeds and green chilli. Set this batter aside.

3. To make the lime pickle yoghurt, spoon the lime pickle into a bowl and mix in the yoghurt.

4. Place a large, non-stick frying pan (skillet) over a medium heat and add just enough oil to coat the bottom of the pan.

5. When the oil is hot, add spoonfuls of the batter to form pancakes roughly 7–8cm (2½–3 inches) in diameter. (The batter will make 4–5 pancakes, so cook in batches to avoid overcrowding the pan.) Cook for 2 minutes, until bubbles have appeared and the batter has set. Flip the pancakes over for a few seconds, then transfer to a plate and keep warm. Repeat this step as necessary to use up the batter, adding a thin layer of oil each time.

6. Serve the pancakes on a platter sprinkled with the coriander leaves, offering the lime pickle yoghurt and lime wedges on the side.

IF YOU HAVE MORE TIME...
...serve with a simple Indian katchumber salad: mix together thick slices of cucumber, diced tomato and sliced onion and dress with coriander leaves and lime juice to taste.

Japanese-style noodle omelette with crab, barbecue ketchup and Kewpie mayonnaise

The Japanese name for this fritter-like omelette is okonomiyaki, which means 'how you like it cooked', so there are lots of regional variations across Japan. If you don't eat crab, you can leave it out or swap it for crispy bacon, cooked shrimps or chargrilled squid. Kewpie is the number one brand of mayonnaise in Japan, and it's widely available across the United States, but less so in the UK, where you will have to track it down online or replace with regular mayo. Serve the omelette with edamame, steamed spinach or Asian greens.

4 eggs
3 heaped tbsp plain
   (all-purpose) flour
100g (4oz) fresh egg noodles
100g (1½ cups) finely shredded
   white cabbage
2 spring onions (scallions),
   roughly chopped
2 tbsp vegetable oil, for frying
Sea salt and freshly ground
   black pepper

For the barbecue ketchup
2 tsp clear honey
2 tsp tomato ketchup
2 tsp soy sauce
2 tsp Worcestershire sauce

To serve
60g (2½oz) picked white crab
   meat (optional)
2 tbsp crispy fried onions
2 tbsp coriander (cilantro)
   leaves
½ red or green chilli, deseeded
   if you want a milder heat,
   sliced (optional)
2 tbsp Kewpie mayonnaise

1. Crack the eggs into a bowl and add the flour. Whisk together until smooth.

2. Add the noodles, cabbage and spring onions to the batter and mix together. Season with salt and pepper.

3. Place a non-stick frying pan (skillet) over a medium heat and add a tablespoon of oil. When hot, pour the noodle mixture into the pan and allow to cook for 4 minutes.

4. Meanwhile, make the barbecue ketchup by putting all the ingredients into a bowl and mixing thoroughly.

5. Using a board or plate to help you, flip the omelette and continue to cook the other side for 2 minutes.

6. Carefully slide the omelette onto a plate and dress the top with the crab meat (if using), the crispy onions, coriander leaves and fresh chilli (if using).

7. To serve, drizzle the top with zigzags of the barbecue ketchup and the mayonnaise.

Spinach and feta böreks with cucumber raita

The trick to making these spinach and feta parcels in ten minutes is using spring roll (egg roll) wrappers, or, to give this pastry its proper name, *feuille de brick*. It's similar to filo pastry, but easier to handle, quicker to cook and less likely to crack during the cooking. If you have the time and extra ingredients, make as many of these as you can – you won't regret being able to go back for more!

150g (5oz) frozen leaf spinach, defrosted
70g (½ cup) crumbled feta cheese or vegetarian equivalent
2 tbsp roughly chopped dill
Zest of 1 lemon
Pinch of chilli flakes
1 tbsp plain (all-purpose) flour
4 spring roll (egg roll) wrappers
Olive oil, for frying
1 tbsp sesame seeds or mixed linseed, pumpkin and sunflower seeds

For the raita
½ small cucumber
1 garlic clove, peeled
1 tbsp roughly chopped dill
1 tbsp chopped mint leaves
60g (¼ cup) Greek yoghurt
Juice of 1 lemon

1. Squeeze any excess water out of the spinach, then put it in a bowl with the feta, dill, lemon zest and chilli flakes and stir to combine.

2. Mix the flour with just enough water to make a thin but not runny paste. Lay a spring roll wrapper on a chopping board, then brush it with the flour paste and stick a second wrapper on top.

3. Put half the spinach mixture in the centre of the double wrapper and, working clockwise, fold the edges over the filling to form a circle, sticking any overlapping parts down with flour paste. Repeat this step to make another börek.

4. Place a non-stick frying pan (skillet) over a medium heat and coat the bottom with a little olive oil.

5. Brush the seam-free side of the böreks with some of the flour paste and sprinkle with seeds. Place the böreks in the pan, seed-side down, and cook for 3 minutes. Turn them over and cook for a further 3 minutes, or until golden brown.

6. While the böreks are cooking, make the raita: grate the cucumber and garlic into a bowl, add the dill and mint, then the yoghurt and lemon juice, and mix thoroughly.

7. Remove the böreks from the pan and drain on kitchen paper (paper towel) before serving on a board or platter with the raita.

CHEF'S TIP
To get more juice out of a lemon, heat it in the microwave for 20 seconds on full power before squeezing it. The heat helps to break down the membranes in the fruit, which means the juice is released more easily.

Polenta and sweetcorn fritters with fried eggs, avocado and chorizo

Sweetcorn fritters always remind me of trips down under, where the Australians have perfected the art of brunch. Is it all that sunshine, the laid-back lifestyle or the amazing ingredients? I don't know, but I want a bit of what they're having. You can swap the chorizo for some crisped-up rashers of smoky bacon, or leave it out for a vegetarian breakfast. Add kale or spinach to the batter if you want to up the veg content.

10 eggs
200ml (¾ cup) whole milk
220g (scant 2 cups) plain (all-purpose) flour
120g (¾ cup) polenta
400g (scant 3 cups) canned or frozen sweetcorn, drained or defrosted
40g (2 cups) rocket (arugula) or baby spinach
Vegetable oil, for frying
1 avocado
2 spring onions (scallions)
240g (8½oz) sliced chorizo
½ bunch of coriander (cilantro)
Sea salt and freshly ground black pepper

1. Crack six of the eggs into a blender, add the milk, flour, polenta and half the sweetcorn and blitz until combined but still coarse.

2. Pour the mixture into a bowl and fold in the remaining sweetcorn and half the rocket or spinach.

3. Place a large, non-stick frying pan (skillet) over a medium–high heat and add just enough oil to lightly coat the bottom of it.

4. Meanwhile, peel and chop the avocado and roughly chop the spring onions.

5. When the oil is hot, place four separate spoonfuls of the corn mixture in the pan and cook for 2 minutes on each side.

6. Meanwhile, put the chorizo into a different frying pan and cook gently over a low–medium heat, until the fat begins to render and the chorizo starts to crisp.

7. Transfer the chorizo to a plate and keep warm. Return the oily pan to the heat until it is medium hot. Crack in the four remaining eggs and fry for 2–3 minutes, until the whites are firm but the yolks are still runny.

8. When the fritters are cooked, drain them on kitchen paper (paper towel) before placing on two plates. Put the eggs on top, then dress with the remaining rocket leaves, the avocado, spring onions and coriander before spooning the chorizo and chorizo oil over the top.

GF

V

Green polenta with spring vegetables and goats' cheese

You will need to buy quick-cook polenta to get this dish on the table in ten minutes, but any polenta will work if you have more time. You could also use American grits, which are very similar, but made from ground white corn rather than yellow corn, so are lighter in colour and have a slightly different texture. When in season, add wild garlic leaves, sorrel or chive flowers to the vegetable mix.

790ml (3 cups + 2 tbsp) vegetable stock

170g (1 cup) quick-cook polenta

120g (1 stick) soft butter

Scant 3 tbsp freshly grated Parmesan cheese or vegetarian equivalent

1 garlic clove

250g (9oz) frozen chopped spinach, defrosted

70g (⅓ cup) mascarpone cheese

200g (7oz) purple sprouting broccoli

250g (9oz) mixture of broad (fava) beans, peas and/or sugarsnap peas

3 tbsp olive oil

1 tbsp mint leaves

Zest and juice of 1 lemon

120g (4½oz) goats' cheese

Sea salt

1. Pour the stock into a saucepan and bring to the boil.

2. When boiling, add the polenta to the pan in a steady stream and whisk thoroughly. Add the butter and Parmesan and mix with a wooden spoon until both have melted.

3. Peel and crush (mince) or grate the garlic. Add to the polenta along with the spinach and keep cooking for 1 minute. Season with salt and fold in the mascarpone. Remove from the heat.

4. Fill the kettle with water and bring to the boil. Pour it into a large saucepan over a medium heat. When the water is boiling again, add a pinch of salt and the broccoli. Allow to cook for 1½ minutes, then add the mixed beans and peas. Allow to cook for a further 1½ minutes, then drain in a colander.

5. Put the cooked vegetables into a large bowl and add the olive oil, mint leaves, lemon zest and juice, then toss to combine.

6. Spoon the polenta onto four plates, arrange the vegetables over the top, then add slices of the goats' cheese before serving.

Bacon cauliflower cheese on toast

Cheese on toast is made for customising – add a pinch of freshly grated nutmeg to the cheese sauce (leaving out the paprika or cayenne), spread the toast with wholegrain mustard before layering, or stir through some caramelised onions. You can swap the Cheddar for Gruyère, Comté or any cheese that melts well, or make it vegetarian by leaving out the bacon.

100g (½ cup) bacon lardons
210g (2 cups) cauliflower florets (flowerets)
4–6 thick slices of sourdough bread
3 tbsp butter
2 tbsp cream cheese, softened
120ml (½ cup) double (heavy) cream
75g (¾ cup) grated Cheddar cheese
1½ tbsp freshly grated Parmesan cheese
1 tsp mustard
Pinch of paprika or cayenne pepper (optional)
Sea salt and freshly ground black pepper
Chopped chives, to serve

1. Preheat the grill (broiler) to high and line a baking (cookie) sheet with foil.

2. Put a large frying pan (skillet) over a high heat and add the bacon lardons. Stirring frequently, allow to cook for 3–4 minutes, until crisp. Set aside half the bacon for serving.

3. Meanwhile, roughly chop the cauliflower florets into bite-sized pieces.

4. Put the slices of bread on the baking sheet and place under the grill until lightly toasted on just one side.

5. Add the butter to the frying pan and stir through the bacon as it melts. Add the cauliflower, season with salt and pepper and cook for 1–2 minutes, until the butter begins to brown and the cauliflower starts to soften.

6. Stir in the cream cheese and cream, mixing until thick and thoroughly combined.

7. Add half the Cheddar and Parmesan, followed by the mustard and stir until the cheese has melted, adding a little more cream if necessary. Remove the pan from the heat.

8. Flip the slices of toast and spoon the cheesy cauliflower over the untoasted sides. Sprinkle the remaining cheese over the top, add a pinch of paprika or cayenne pepper (if using), and place under the grill for 2 minutes, until golden and bubbling.

9. Scatter the reserved bacon and chopped chives over the top before serving.

TIP FOR SPEED

When you are grating cheese, grate it onto a plate rather than a chopping board. It's much quicker and easier to tip the cheese into the pan, and you don't leave half of it behind.

Smoked salmon omelette Arnold Bennett

Omelette Arnold Bennett was created for the famous novelist of that name by the chef at the Savoy Hotel in London almost a hundred years ago, and it's still on our menu at the Savoy Grill today, not just because of the history, but also because it's totally delicious. Traditionally, it's made with fresh smoked haddock poached in milk and topped with béchamel sauce, but this version is made with a cheat's white sauce and smoked salmon, making it lighter and quicker, but no less tasty.

3½ tbsp whole milk
50g (¼ cup) cream cheese
1 bay leaf
Pinch of freshly grated nutmeg
100g (4oz) smoked or regular Cheddar cheese
4 large eggs, plus 2 egg yolks
50g (scant ½ stick) butter
3½ tbsp double (heavy) cream
85g (3½oz) smoked salmon pieces
1 tbsp chopped dill
Sea salt and freshly ground black pepper

To serve
1 tsp miniature capers
1 tsp chopped chives

1. Preheat the grill (broiler) to high.

2. Pour the milk into a small saucepan and stir in the cream cheese. Add the bay leaf and nutmeg, then place the pan over a medium heat and bring to a simmer. Meanwhile, grate the cheese.

3. Remove the pan from the heat and add half the cheese. Stir until melted, then pour into a bowl and whisk in the egg yolks.

4. Place a small, non-stick frying pan (skillet) over a medium heat and add the butter.

5. Whisk the whole eggs and cream together in a bowl, then pour into the pan. Allow the eggs to cook for 2–3 minutes, stirring regularly with a spatula.

6. Remove the pan from the heat, fold in the smoked salmon and dill, and season with salt and pepper.

7. Divide the omelette between two heatproof serving dishes and pour over the cheese sauce. Sprinkle with the remaining Cheddar and place under the grill until the cheese begins to colour.

8. Sprinkle with the capers and chives before serving.

Chilli quesadillas with grilled avocado and burnt lime crème fraîche

The beauty of these quesadillas is that they're made with lots of ready-to-go ingredients, including soft tortillas, canned black beans, roasted red peppers and sliced jalapeños from a jar. You can also buy pre-grated cheese to make it even less work. You hardly have to cook anything! Dial the heat up or down by adding more or less chilli, depending on who you are feeding.

160g (5½oz) roasted red (bell) peppers, from a jar
2 spring onions (scallions)
2 tbsp sliced green jalapeño chillies, from a jar, plus extra to serve (optional)
1 x 400g (15oz) can of black beans, drained and rinsed
¼ bunch of coriander (cilantro) leaves
4 large corn tortillas
2 tbsp chipotle paste
300g (3 cups) grated cheese (Cheddar, Monterey Jack or mozzarella)
1 avocado
2 limes
6 tbsp crème fraîche (sour cream)

TIP FOR SPEED

To peel avocados quickly, cut them in half and scoop out the stone, then slip a dessertspoon between the flesh and the skin and run it gently around the fruit, keeping the back of the spoon as close to the skin as possible. The flesh should pop out easily.

1. Roughly chop the roasted peppers and spring onions, and mix in a bowl with the sliced jalapeños and black beans.

2. Pick the leaves from the coriander stalks and put them to one side. Finely chop the stalks and add them to the bean mixture.

3. Using a potato masher, crush the beans until the mixture begins to stick together but is still chunky.

4. Lay two of the tortillas on a work surface and spread them with a layer of chipotle paste, leaving a clear border all around the edge. Divide the bean mixture equally between the tortillas and spread it over the paste.

5. Sprinkle the cheese over the beans and put the remaining tortillas on top to make quesadillas.

6. Place two non-stick frying pans (skillets) over a medium heat and, when hot, cook the quesadillas for 2–3 minutes on each side.

7. Meanwhile, slice around the avocado, remove the stone and peel off the skin (see tip). Cut each half of flesh in half again, so you have 4 quarters. Place a non-stick frying pan or griddle (grill) pan over a high heat and cook the avocado until blackened on all sides.

8. Cut the limes in half and place them flesh-side down in the hot avocado pan until charred. Put the crème fraîche into a bowl and squeeze in the juice of the charred limes. Stir well to combine.

9. Slice the quesadillas into wedges, then put the avocado quarters and a spoonful of crème fraîche on top. Scatter the coriander leaves and extra sliced chillies (if using) over the quesadillas before serving.

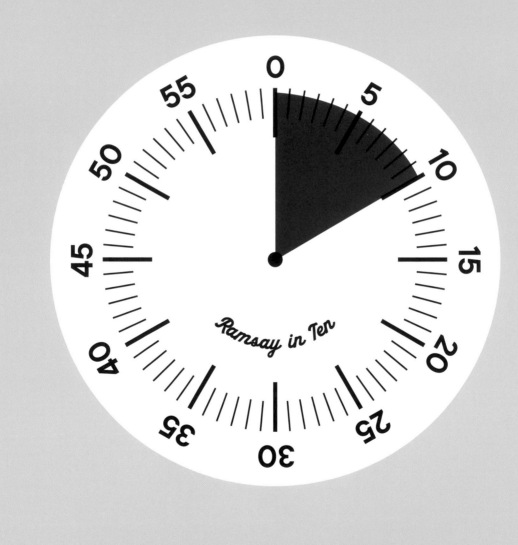

PASTA, RICE & NOODLES

Super green pasta with rocket, almonds and lemon

This is a really easy way to boost your intake of cruciferous greens – that's kale and rocket (arugula) to you and me. You could add broccoli or spinach to make it even more nutritious, and use wholewheat pasta, if you have more time. Serve with a tomato salad to balance out all that greenness, and leave out the anchovy and Parmesan if you want to make it vegan.

4 tbsp olive oil, plus extra
   for drizzling
3 garlic cloves
2 anchovy fillets (optional,
   leave out if cooking
   vegetarian)
250g (3½ cups) chopped kale
500g (1lb 2oz) fresh pasta
   (any type)
60g (¼ cup) roasted almonds
1 lemon
6 tbsp freshly grated
   Parmesan cheese or
   vegetarian equivalent
2 large handfuls of rocket
   (arugula)
Sea salt and freshly ground
   black pepper

1. Fill the kettle with water and bring to the boil, then pour into a large saucepan, season with salt and return to the boil.

2. Place another large saucepan over a medium heat and add the measured olive oil.

3. Peel and finely slice the garlic, add to the oil and cook for 2 minutes, until lightly coloured. Add the anchovies (if using) and break them down with a wooden spoon.

4. Add the kale to the pan, along with a spoonful of the boiling water, cover with a lid and steam for 3 minutes.

5. Put the pasta into the pan of boiling water and stir to separate. Cook for 2 minutes, or as per the packet instructions.

6. Roughly chop the almonds and zest the lemon.

7. Remove the kale from the heat and, using a hand-held blender, blitz until smooth.

8. Drain the pasta and add it to the kale along with the lemon zest, half the Parmesan and some salt and pepper. Toss together.

9. Divide between four bowls and finish with the rocket, almonds, remaining Parmesan and a drizzle of olive oil.

One-pan pumpkin pasta with amaretti biscuits and lemon thyme

Not only is this sauce cooked in the same time as the pasta, it's also cooked in the same pan, meaning less fuss and less washing up at the end – always a result in my house. Sprinkling amaretti biscuits over the top might seem bizarre, but the hint of sweetness and the almond flavour finish the dish beautifully. Leave them out if you prefer. You could also stir through some shredded cooked chicken, if you have some.

3 tbsp olive oil

1 banana shallot (echalion) or 2 regular shallots

150g (5oz) orzo pasta

200g (1¾ cups) diced pumpkin

750ml (3 cups) boiling vegetable stock

100g (4oz) purple sprouting broccoli

60g (½ stick) butter

1 tbsp freshly grated Parmesan cheese or vegetarian equivalent

4 amaretti biscuits (cookies), crushed

¼ bunch of lemon thyme, leaves picked

Chilli flakes, to serve (optional)

1. Place a heavy-based saucepan over a medium heat and add 2 tablespoons of the olive oil.

2. While the oil is heating up, peel and slice the shallot. Add to the pan and sweat for 1 minute.

3. Add the orzo and pumpkin and cook for a further minute.

4. Add a third of the stock to the pan and cover with a lid. Cook for 2 minutes, then add more stock. Repeat every 2 minutes until the orzo has absorbed all the stock.

5. Meanwhile, trim the broccoli, and when the orzo has been cooking for 6–7 minutes, add it to the pan. Cook for 2 more minutes, then remove from the heat.

6. Stir in the butter and remaining tablespoon olive oil, followed by the Parmesan.

7. Allow to rest for 2 minutes, then sprinkle with the crushed amaretti, lemon thyme and chilli flakes (if using) before serving.

CHEF'S TIP
Buy ready-peeled and chopped pumpkin to minimize the prep time.

**SERVES 2
(OR 4 AS A STARTER)**

Basil gnudi with fresh tomato sauce

Gnudi are a bit like gnocchi, but they are made from ricotta cheese and semolina instead of potato. It might seem daunting to make them at home, but trust me, they're really easy and they will take less time to put together than boiling a pan of spuds! Ricotta salata is ricotta that has been salted and aged so that it is firm enough to grate or crumble. If you can't find it, use pecorino or Parmesan instead.

250g (1 cup) ricotta cheese
2 eggs
120g (1 cup) plain (all-purpose) flour, plus extra for dusting
4 tbsp freshly grated Parmesan cheese or vegetarian equivalent
1 tsp sea salt
⅓ bunch of basil
2 tbsp olive oil, plus extra for drizzling
2 garlic cloves
180g (1 generous cup) cherry tomatoes
70g (⅓ cup) butter
30g (1oz) ricotta salata, pecorino or Parmesan cheese
Freshly ground black pepper

1. Put the ricotta, eggs, flour, Parmesan and salt into a bowl and mix until a smooth dough forms.

2. Roughly chop half the basil and mix it through the gnudi dough.

3. Dust a board or clean work surface with flour, then divide the dough into four equal pieces. With floured hands, roll each piece into seven walnut-sized balls. These are your gnudi.

4. Fill the kettle with water and bring to the boil, then pour it into a saucepan, season with salt and return to the boil.

5. Place another saucepan over a medium heat and add the measured olive oil. While it is heating, peel and slice the garlic, then add it to the pan and cook until it starts to sizzle.

6. Cut the tomatoes in half and add them to the garlic. Continue to cook for 3 minutes, until soft. Add the butter to the pan and stir through as it melts.

7. When the pan of water is boiling, add the gnudi. Once they start to float, cook for 2 minutes.

8. Add 2–3 spoonfuls of the starchy water to the tomato sauce and stir to combine.

9. Drain the gnudi and add them to the sauce. Toss to coat, then season with black pepper.

10. Divide between four warm bowls and finish with a sprinkle of the remaining basil leaves and a grating of ricotta salata or pecorino. Drizzle with olive oil before serving.

Warung-style fried noodles

A warung is a kerb-side restaurant or food stall in Indonesia that usually has a long queue outside. On the menu? Simple, traditional street food, such as *nasi goreng* (fried rice) and *mie goreng* (fried noodles) with pork, chicken or prawns, all cooked very fast with plenty of heat, spice and smoke. Making fried noodles like this at home is quick and easy, and you don't even need to queue.

4 tbsp soy sauce or tamari

2 tbsp oyster sauce

3 tbsp coconut palm sugar or dark brown sugar

1 tbsp ground coriander

2 tsp ginger paste

2 tsp garlic paste

2–3 heads of Asian greens (pak choi/bok choy or choi sum/choy sum)

2 spring onions (scallions)

125g (4½oz) streaky (American) bacon

2 tbsp vegetable oil, plus extra for frying

2 eggs

225g (8oz) cooked flat rice noodles

100g (1 cup) beansprouts, ready to eat

To serve

1 tbsp coriander (cilantro) leaves

Pinch of shichimi togarashi seasoning (optional)

1. Put the soy sauce, oyster sauce, sugar, ground coriander, ginger and garlic pastes into a bowl and whisk together until you have a smooth sauce.

2. Slice the Asian greens into 5cm (2 inch) pieces and roughly chop the spring onions.

3. Place a wok over a high heat until smoking hot, meanwhile cutting the bacon into 2.5cm (1 inch) strips. Add a little oil to the hot wok, then reduce the heat to medium–high and add the bacon. Cook for 1 minute, then add the 2 tablespoons oil to the wok. Once shimmering, crack in the eggs and cook for 30 seconds, breaking them up slightly with a spatula. Move to the side of the wok and add the noodles. Allow them to cook undisturbed for 30 seconds – they should start to char.

4. Add the sauce to the wok, stir to combine with the eggs and noodles, and bring to the boil. Add the Asian greens, spring onions and beansprouts to the pan and toss to combine, then cook for 1–2 minutes, pressing everything into the sides of the pan to char and caramelise.

5. Divide between two bowls and top with the coriander leaves and a pinch of togarashi (if using).

Quick mushroom lasagne

I know, I know, it seems unlikely that you can cook a lasagne in ten minutes, but this isn't any ordinary lasagne. It's made with fresh lasagne sheets and an instant white sauce made from cream cheese and cream, which is as delicious as it sounds. A mixture of different mushroom varieties gives the best flavour, so choose from a selection of chestnut (cremini), portobello, shiitake, oyster or button, depending on what you can get hold of.

225g (8oz) cream cheese, at room temperature
500ml (2 cups) double (heavy) cream
2 tbsp thyme leaves
Olive oil, for frying
350g (12oz) mixed mushrooms
2 garlic cloves
1 shallot
3 tbsp butter
85ml (⅓ cup) dry white wine
2–3 handfuls of fresh spinach or sliced kale/Swiss chard
225g (8oz) fresh lasagne sheets
175g (1½ cups) grated mozzarella cheese
50g (½ cup) finely grated pecorino or Parmesan cheese or vegetarian equivalent
Sea salt and freshly ground black pepper
Small handful of chopped basil, to serve

1. Put the cream cheese, double cream and thyme leaves into a bowl and whisk together until smooth.

2. Place an ovenproof frying pan (skillet) over a high heat and add enough oil to coat the bottom generously.

3. Slice the mushrooms into bite-sized pieces.

4. When the oil is hot, add the mushrooms, cover and cook for 2 minutes.

5. Meanwhile, peel and grate or finely chop the garlic and shallot.

6. Add the butter, garlic and shallot to the mushrooms and season with salt and pepper. Cook for 2 minutes, then deglaze the pan with the wine. Bring to the boil and reduce the liquid by half, then add half the cream cheese sauce, stirring to combine.

7. Add the spinach to the pan and stir through.

8. Cut the lasagne into 7.5cm (3 inch) squares and push half of them into the sauce with a wooden spoon until they are covered. Arrange the remaining squares on top and spoon the remaining cheese sauce over them. Sprinkle with half the grated cheese, then cover the pan, reduce the heat to medium and allow to simmer for 4–5 minutes.

9. Meanwhile, preheat the grill (broiler) to high.

10. Remove the lid and sprinkle the remaining cheese over the top. Place under the grill for 1–2 minutes, until golden and bubbling.

11. Sprinkle with the chopped basil and serve immediately.

CHEF'S TIP
Blanch the lasagne sheets in boiling water for a few seconds before inserting into the sauce; this will make them a little easier to handle and even quicker to cook.

Tuna puttanesca with black olive gremolata

It's always good to have a store-cupboard standby up your sleeve, and puttanesca is one of the greatest. Throw in a tin of tuna to make it more substantial and extra nutritious, but always make sure you buy good-quality, sustainably sourced tuna in olive oil – the finished dish will thank you for it. Any fresh or dried pasta will work, so go with whatever you have in your cupboard.

1 tbsp olive oil, plus extra
   for drizzling
2 garlic cloves
1 tsp chopped red chilli or
   ½ tsp dry chilli flakes
4 anchovy fillets
1 x 400g (15oz) can of
   chopped tomatoes
400–500g (14–18oz) fresh
   pasta, e.g. paccheri or fusilli,
   or 300g (11oz) dried pasta
Juice of 1 lemon
1 tsp fine capers
1 x 145g (5oz) can of tuna
Sea salt and freshly ground
   black pepper

For the olive gremolata
Zest of 1 lemon
30g (½ cup) finely chopped
   parsley leaves, plus a few
   whole leaves to garnish
6 pitted black olives, chopped

1. Place a large, non-stick frying pan (skillet) over a high heat and coat the bottom of the pan with a thin layer of oil. Meanwhile, peel and crush (mince) or grate the garlic. Add it to the hot oil, toast a little, then add the chilli and anchovies. Use a spoon to crush the anchovies to a paste and allow to cook for 1 minute.

2. Add the tomatoes, season with salt and pepper and stir well, then reduce the heat and leave to simmer until needed.

3. Make the olive gremolata by mixing all the ingredients for it in a bowl.

4. Fill the kettle with water and bring to the boil, then pour it into a saucepan, season with salt and return to the boil.

5. Add the pasta to the water and stir to separate. Cook for 2 minutes, or as per the packet instructions.

6. Drain the pasta, reserving a little of the water. Add the pasta and reserved water to the tomato sauce and toss to coat.

7. Stir in the lemon juice, capers and tuna, then spoon into bowls.

8. Top each serving with a spoonful of the gremolata, a drizzle of olive oil and parsley leaves.

Sardine and fennel linguine with pine nuts, raisins and capers

This combination of fish, fennel, pine nuts, raisins and capers comes straight from the kitchens of Sicily, where they have perfected the art of balancing sweet, tart and salty ingredients. It is one of those dishes that turns out to be much more than the sum of its parts flavour-wise, and really easy to boot. Get the fishmonger to butterfly the sardines, or use fillets if that isn't an option.

3 tbsp raisins
Pinch of saffron threads
85ml (⅓ cup) dry white wine
8 sardine fillets
1 tsp chilli flakes
1 tsp fennel seeds
2 tbsp olive oil, plus extra
  for drizzling
3 tbsp pine nuts
3 anchovy fillets
500g (1lb 2oz) fresh linguine
Small handful of flat-leaf
  parsley
3 tbsp baby capers
Zest of 1 lemon
Sea salt

1. Put the raisins and saffron into a small bowl, add the wine and leave to soak.

2. Fill the kettle with water and bring to the boil, then pour into a saucepan, season with salt and return to the boil.

3. Place a frying pan (skillet) over a medium heat. Season the sardine flesh with salt, chilli flakes and fennel seeds, then place in the hot pan, skin-side down. Allow to cook for 30 seconds.

4. Carefully add a splash of olive oil, then add the pine nuts and cook until toasted. Add the anchovies and break them down with a wooden spoon.

5. Put the linguine into the boiling water. Stir to separate, then allow to cook for 2 minutes, or as per the packet instructions.

6. Roughly chop the parsley and add to the sardine pan along with the capers, lemon zest and contents of the wine bowl.

7. Drain the pasta, tip into a large bowl with the sardine mixture and toss to combine. Add a drizzle of olive oil, and serve with crispy fennel breadcrumbs (see below) if you like.

IF YOU HAVE MORE TIME...
...make crispy fennel breadcrumbs to scatter over the finished dish: toast 6 tablespoons breadcrumbs with 1 teaspoon fennel seeds in 2 tablespoons olive oil over a medium heat until crisp and golden brown.

Quick smoked haddock kedgeree

Making a classic kedgeree (an Anglo-Indian smoked fish and curried rice dish) can take about 45 minutes, but this sped-up version with pre-cooked rice is on the table in around ten, making it a brilliant hangover brunch or last-minute supper. Try to find haddock that has been traditionally smoked over wood chips rather than industrially flavoured – the difference is incredible. You could also use salmon here, or lose the fish altogether and try my Vedgeree on page 73.

2 eggs
300g (11oz) undyed smoked haddock or smoked cod, skinned
2 tbsp butter
1 tsp grated fresh ginger
½ tsp curry powder
2 cardamom pods
½ tsp ground turmeric
100ml (scant ½ cup) double (heavy) cream
100ml (scant ½ cup) whole milk
250g (1½ cups) cooked basmati rice
Sea salt and freshly ground black pepper

To serve
1 tbsp chopped flat-leaf parsley
2 tbsp crispy fried onions
Lime pickle
Natural (plain) yoghurt

1. Fill the kettle with water and bring to the boil, then pour it into a small saucepan and return to the boil. Add the eggs and cook for 8 minutes.

2. Meanwhile, put the fish into a steamer, cover it and place on top of the egg pan, then steam for 6 minutes. (If you don't have a steamer, grill or shallow-poach the fish for the same amount of time.)

3. Melt the butter in a saucepan over a medium heat, add the ginger, curry powder, cardamom pods and turmeric and warm through.

4. Stir the cream and milk into the pan. When warm, add the rice. Season with salt and pepper, stir well and allow to cook for 2 minutes, until hot.

5. When the eggs are cooked, remove from the pan and shell them under cold running water. Cut into quarters.

6. Carefully remove the fish from steamer, break the flesh into pieces and fold through the rice.

7. Transfer the rice mixture to a serving dish and place the eggs on top. Scatter over the chopped parsley and crispy onions, and season with a few twists of black pepper. Serve with the lime pickle and yoghurt on the side.

Creamy cannellini pasta with spicy salami and walnut topping

This is a creamy pasta sauce without any cream: the velvety texture of the cannellini beans and the starchy pasta water combine to coat the pasta without needing any dairy to bind it. The salami and walnut topping is optional, as the pasta is really great without it, and including it might push you over the ten-minute mark, but it does make the dish extra delicious.

175g (6oz) penne, farfalle or conchiglie
3–4 tbsp olive oil
2 garlic cloves
2 sprigs of rosemary, leaves picked
1 x 400g (15oz) can of cannellini beans, drained and rinsed
60ml (¼ cup) white wine
180g (2 cups) chopped cavolo nero (lacinato kale)
85ml (⅓ cup) chicken or vegetable stock
2 tbsp butter
Sea salt and freshly ground black pepper
Shaved pecorino or Parmesan cheese, to serve

For the spicy salami and walnut topping
50g (2oz) sliced salami, cut into thin strips
1 garlic clove
2 tbsp walnuts, chopped
2 tbsp olive oil
1 tbsp nduja

1. Fill the kettle with water and bring to the boil. Pour it into a saucepan, season with salt and return to the boil. Add the pasta and cook for 8–9 minutes, until al dente.

2. Meanwhile, place a large saucepan or flameproof casserole dish (Dutch oven) over a medium–high heat and add the olive oil.

3. While the oil is heating, peel and crush (mince) or grate the garlic and chop the rosemary, then add them to the oil and fry for 20–30 seconds.

4. Add the beans to the pan and season with salt and pepper. Fry for 2–3 minutes, until they start to caramelise, stirring with a wooden spoon to stop them catching.

5. Add the wine and bring to the boil, regularly scraping the bottom of the pan, until the wine is reduced by about half.

6. Meanwhile, prepare the salami and walnut topping: place a frying pan (skillet) over a medium–high heat and fry the salami for 1 minute. Peel and finely grate the garlic, then add to the pan along with the walnuts and olive oil and cook for 2 minutes, until toasted and fragrant. Stir through the nduja and allow to cook until the liquid has totally reduced, then remove from the heat.

7. Using a potato masher or the back of a large spoon, roughly mash most of the beans, then add the cavolo nero and stock to the pan and bring to the boil.

8. Drain the pasta, reserving half a mug of the water. Add the pasta and butter to the beans and toss well, adding a little more stock if you want to thin the sauce, or some of the pasta water to enhance the creaminess.

9. Divide between two bowls and dress with pecorino or Parmesan shavings and the salami and walnut topping.

Cornish 'carbonara' with chilli, mushrooms and peas

I'm using the term 'carbonara' loosely here to describe a pasta dish I cooked during lockdown in Cornwall, when access to the finest Italian pancetta and three-year-old Parmigiano Reggiano was somewhat limited. Instead, my Cornish version uses ingredients you always have in the kitchen, such as bacon lardons, button mushrooms and frozen peas. It might not be authentic, but who cares when it's this delicious?

225g (8oz) spaghetti

Olive oil, for frying

175g (6oz) smoked bacon lardons

2 garlic cloves

100g (4oz) mixed mushrooms

1 small red chilli, deseeded if you want a milder heat (optional)

25g (1oz) Parmesan cheese

3 egg yolks

75g (⅓ cup) crème fraîche (sour cream)

75g (½ cup) frozen peas, defrosted

Sea salt and freshly ground black pepper

To serve

Roughly chopped flat-leaf parsley

Freshly grated Parmesan cheese

1. Fill the kettle with water and bring to the boil, then pour it into a saucepan, season with salt and return to the boil. Add the pasta and cook for 7–9 minutes, until al dente.

2. Meanwhile, place a large, non-stick frying pan (skillet) over a medium–high heat and add a little olive oil. When hot, add the bacon and allow to cook for 3–4 minutes, until crisp. Season with pepper.

3. While the bacon is cooking, peel and grate or crush (mince) the garlic, slice the mushrooms and chop the chilli (if using).

4. Add the garlic to the frying pan and allow to cook for about 30 seconds, before adding the mushrooms and chilli (if using), and seasoning with salt and pepper. Allow to cook for 2–3 minutes.

5. Grate the Parmesan directly onto the egg yolks in a small bowl, then add the crème fraîche and a splash of water and stir to combine.

6. Add the peas to the bacon mixture and toss to combine, then add a few large spoonfuls (about one-third of a mug/cup) of pasta water to the frying pan and toss again.

7. Drain the pasta in a colander, reserving about half a mug (cup) of pasta water, then add the spaghetti and reserved water to the frying pan and toss to combine.

8. Lower the heat and pour the egg mixture into the pan, tossing quickly to gently cook it.

9. Stir in the parsley, then transfer to plates or bowls and sprinkle with Parmesan before serving.

Vedgeree

Do you see what I did there? All the flavour and comfort of a kedgeree but without the fish. You can add more and different vegetables to this version, such as peas, baby spinach, kale, green beans or broccoli, depending on what you have in the fridge, and, if you aren't vegan, a couple of boiled or poached eggs would be a great addition too. Serve with coconut yoghurt and lime pickle on the side.

3 tbsp olive oil
150g (5oz) firm tofu
½ tsp curry powder
2 cardamom pods
½ tsp ground turmeric
1 tsp freshly grated ginger
125ml (½ cup) boiling
  vegetable stock
250g (1½ cups) cooked
  basmati rice
120g (4½oz) sun blush
  tomatoes
2 nori sheets
Sea salt and freshly ground
  black pepper

To serve
1 tbsp chopped flat-leaf
  parsley leaves
Chopped fresh chilli,
  deseeded if you want
  a milder heat (optional)
2 tbsp crispy fried onions
Lime pickle
Coconut yoghurt

1. Place a non-stick frying pan (skillet) over a medium heat and add a tablespoon of the olive oil.

2. Cut the tofu into 3cm (1¼ inch) cubes and add to the pan. Cook for 2 minutes, flipping regularly, until golden brown.

3. Meanwhile, put the remaining 2 tablespoons olive oil into a saucepan and place over a medium heat. Add the curry powder, cardamom pods and turmeric, then stir in the grated ginger.

4. Pour the boiling stock over the spices, add the rice and stir well. Cook for 2–3 minutes, until the rice is hot.

5. Add the tomatoes to the pan of tofu and heat through for 1–2 minutes.

6. Rip the nori sheets into 3cm (1¼ inch) pieces and fold through the hot rice.

7. Spoon the rice into bowls and place the tofu and tomatoes on top. Scatter over the parsley, chilli (if using) and crispy onions, and season with a few twists of black pepper before serving with the lime pickle and coconut yoghurt on the side.

Turkey and leek fusilli with crispy sage breadcrumbs

For a change, skip the bolognese and make this creamy turkey and leek sauce in a fraction of the time instead. It might just become a regular midweek family meal, as it has at my house. You could also make it with minced (ground) chicken or sausage meat, and you can swap the sage for thyme, parsley or tarragon, depending on your preference. Any shape of fresh or dried pasta would work too.

2 tbsp olive oil, plus extra for drizzling

2 banana shallots (echalion) or 4 regular shallots

3 garlic cloves

4 sage leaves

400g (14oz) minced (ground) turkey leg

2 leeks

480g (17oz) fresh fusilli or penne

200ml (¾ cup) double (heavy) cream

Small handful of flat-leaf parsley leaves

1 lemon

Sea salt and freshly ground black pepper

Freshly grated Parmesan cheese, to serve

For the crispy sage breadcrumbs (optional)

2 tbsp olive oil

2 sage leaves

6 tbsp fresh breadcrumbs

1. Fill the kettle with water and bring to the boil, then pour it into a saucepan, season with salt and return to the boil.

2. Place a large, heavy-based frying pan (skillet) over a medium–high heat and add 2 tablespoons olive oil. While the oil is heating, peel and roughly grate the shallots and garlic, then add to the pan. Allow to cook for 2 minutes, stirring regularly.

3. Add the sage leaves and turkey, breaking up the meat with a wooden spoon while it cooks for 3–4 minutes, until lightly browned.

4. Meanwhile, finely slice the leeks and add to the boiling water for 1 minute, before adding the fusilli. Stir to separate the pasta, then allow to cook for 2 minutes, or as per the packet instructions.

5. Pour the cream into the meat, stir to combine, and allow to come to the boil. Reduce to a simmer until needed.

6. If making the crispy sage breadcrumbs, place a frying pan over a medium heat and add the olive oil. Finely chop the sage leaves, then add them to the hot oil along with the breadcrumbs. Cook until crisp and golden brown.

7. Drain the pasta and leeks, reserving 2–3 tablespoons of the water, and add them to the sauce.

8. Finely chop the parsley leaves and zest the lemon, then add both to the pasta along with some salt and pepper. Stir thoroughly to combine.

9. Divide the pasta between four bowls and finish with the sage breadcrumbs (if making), some freshly grated Parmesan and a drizzle of olive oil.

Cauliflower, ginger and sesame ramen

The success of a bowl of ramen rests on the quality of the broth, and good broth, as we all know, takes a really long cooking time to develop that complexity and depth of flavour. Not true if you're vegan, though. This almost-instant shiitake stock is packed with umami and flavoured with mirin and miso paste, which gives it an amazing intensity in no time at all.

10g dried shiitake mushrooms
140g (2 nests) egg noodles
240g (2½ cups) cauliflower florets (flowerets)
1 tbsp rice flour, for dusting
Vegetable oil, for frying
2 tbsp toasted white sesame seeds, from a jar
2 tbsp sesame oil
80ml (3fl oz) mirin
4 tbsp light soy sauce
80g (3¼oz) white miso paste
1 tbsp chopped ginger, from a jar
150g (⅔ cup) diced tofu

To serve
2 spring onions (scallions), finely sliced
Shichimi togarashi seasoning (optional)
1 lime, quartered

1. Bring 500ml (2 cups) water to a simmer in a small pan, then add the shiitake, remove from the heat and allow to infuse for 8 minutes.

2. Fill the kettle with water and bring to the boil, then pour it over the noodles in a heatproof bowl. Stir to separate the noodles and allow to soak for 4 minutes, or as per the packet instructions.

3. Meanwhile, grate the cauliflower florets, then slice the stalks. Toss all the cauliflower in the rice flour to coat.

4. Place a large, non-stick frying pan (skillet) over a medium–high heat and add a thin layer of vegetable oil. When hot, add the cauliflower and cook for 4–5 minutes, until golden brown. Remove from the pan, drain on kitchen paper (paper towel), then toss with the toasted sesame seeds.

5. Drain the noodles, then season with the sesame oil.

6. Return the stock to a medium heat and stir in the mirin, soy sauce, miso paste and ginger.

7. While the stock mixture is warming, finely slice the spring onions.

8. Put the noodles into two bowls and add the tofu and cauliflower. Pour over the warm stock and dress with the spring onions and a sprinkle of shichimi seasoning (if using) before serving with wedges of lime.

IF YOU HAVE MORE TIME...

...serve the ramen with soft-boiled eggs on top if you're not vegan: simmer 2 eggs in boiling water for 6 minutes. Remove from the pan, cool under cold running water, then peel and cut in half. Place on top of the noodles with the toppings.

Stracci with smoked trout, fennel and samphire

Stracci is the Italian word for 'rags', and in this context it refers to roughly torn pieces of fresh pasta. It's a good way to use up the trimmings left over after making ravioli, but can also be made from scratch in seconds by slicing up a few sheets of ready-made fresh lasagne. You don't have to serve this with fish eggs, but they add a salty kick and burst-in-your-mouth texture to this lovely summery dish.

6 fresh lasagne sheets
80g (3¼oz) baby fennel
40g (⅓ stick) butter
50g (2oz) samphire
  or asparagus tips, trimmed
4 tbsp crème fraîche
  (sour cream)
125g (4½oz) smoked trout,
  flaked
Zest and juice of 1 lemon
Sea salt and freshly ground
  black pepper
Fish eggs (optional), to serve

1. Cut the lasagne sheets into random strips and triangles.

2. Remove any fronds from the fennel and set them aside. Finely slice the fennel bulb by hand or using a mandoline.

3. Place a non-stick frying pan (skillet) over a medium heat and add the butter. When melted, add the sliced fennel and cook for 6–7 minutes, until semi-translucent.

4. Fill the kettle with water and bring to the boil, then pour it into a saucepan, season with salt and return to the boil. When boiling, add the pasta and samphire and cook for 2 minutes.

5. Stir the crème fraîche into the cooked fennel.

6. Drain the pasta and samphire and add to the fennel pan along with the trout, lemon zest and juice. Season with black pepper and toss to combine.

7. Divide between two bowls and top with any reserved fennel fronds before serving with caviar (if using).

CHICKEN
& DUCK

Steamed chicken with quinoa, spiced carrots and green mojo sauce

Mojo sauce originally comes from the Canary Islands, where they serve red or green mojo with almost everything, but particularly with their famous *papas arrugadas* (wrinkly potatoes). Every recipe is different, but the green one is always packed with lots of soft herbs to give it its vibrant colour. My simple version goes beautifully with this steamed chicken salad, but it's also great with fish, pork, steak and, of course, potatoes, wrinkly or otherwise.

4 chicken mini fillets
3 tbsp olive oil
2 carrots
1 orange
1 tbsp dukkah
2 tbsp smoked almonds
250g (1 generous cup) cooked
    quinoa, couscous or lentils
1 tbsp coriander (cilantro)
    leaves
1 tbsp mint leaves
Large handful of mixed baby
    salad leaves
Sea salt and freshly ground
    black pepper

For the mojo sauce
1 tbsp chopped jalapeño
    chilli (from a jar), plus
    1 tbsp of the juice
2 tbsp coriander (cilantro)
    leaves
2 tbsp mint leaves
2 tbsp natural (plain) yoghurt

1. Fill the kettle with water and bring to the boil, then pour it into a saucepan and return to the boil.

2. Put the chicken fillets into a steamer, making sure they don't overlap, then drizzle with 1 tablespoon of the olive oil and season with salt and pepper. Place the steamer over the boiling water, cover with the lid and steam for 6 minutes.

3. Trim the carrots, then grate them or cut into matchsticks.

4. Grate the orange zest over the carrots and squeeze in the orange juice before adding the remaining olive oil and the dukkah.

5. Roughly chop the almonds.

6. Now make the mojo sauce: put the chilli and juice into a small blender, add the coriander and mint and blitz until smooth. Decant into a small bowl and stir in the yoghurt.

7. Season the quinoa with salt and pepper and divide between two bowls. Put the chicken fillets on top and drizzle over the mojo sauce.

8. Fold the herbs and baby leaves through the carrots and place on top of the chicken. Finish with the chopped nuts before serving with any leftover mojo sauce on the side.

Chicken souvlaki flatbreads

Hot, fresh souvlaki is Greek street food at its finest. I use chicken thighs because they are so much juicier than breast, but they take longer to cook, so flattening them beforehand is essential if you want to be quick. As with all yoghurt marinades, the longer you leave the meat in them, the deeper they will penetrate, so if you are not in a hurry, coat the thighs and leave them in the fridge for a couple of hours before cooking.

1 tsp fennel seeds
1 tsp cumin seeds
1 tsp freshly ground
  black pepper
1 tsp dried thyme
4 skinless and boneless
  chicken thighs
4 tbsp natural (plain) yoghurt
  (Greek if you like)
½ garlic clove
1 tsp chopped red chilli,
  deseeded if you want a
  milder heat (optional)

To serve
2 flatbreads
¼ red onion
10cm (4 inch) piece
  of cucumber
1 tsp thyme leaves
Zest of 1 unwaxed lemon

1. Place a griddle (grill) pan over a high heat.

2. Put the fennel and cumin seeds, black pepper and dried thyme into a small, dry frying pan (skillet) over a medium heat until toasted and fragrant.

3. Sandwich the chicken thighs between two sheets of cling film (plastic wrap) or baking (parchment) paper and bash with a meat hammer or rolling pin until they are evenly flattened out to half their original thickness.

4. Put 2 tablespoons of the yoghurt into a large bowl with the toasted spices and mix well. Add the chicken thighs and stir to coat.

5. Weave a metal skewer in and out of each chicken thigh, then place in the hot griddle pan and cook for 3–4 minutes on each side.

6. Meanwhile, peel and crush (mince) or grate the garlic into the remaining yoghurt and stir to combine.

7. Place an empty frying pan over a medium heat and warm the flatbreads for a few seconds each.

8. Peel and finely slice the red onion and cucumber and mix together.

9. Spoon the garlic yoghurt and chopped chilli (if using) onto the flatbreads and place the chicken thighs on top. Garnish with the cucumber and red onion, then sprinkle with the thyme leaves and lemon zest before serving.

CHEF'S TIP
Use metal skewers if you have them, but if wooden skewers are the only option, make sure you soak them in water for at least 30 minutes before cooking or they will burn.

Spiced spatchcock chicken with green goddess dressing

This ambitious recipe, which involves cooking a whole chicken in ten minutes, will only work if you start with a smallish chicken, not a massive one, and use a rectangular griddle (grill) pan large enough to fit the spatchcocked bird. Place the pan over two burners and make sure it is smoking hot before starting. Cooking the chicken *al mattone*, or under a brick, helps to speed up the cooking process. You can use a brick if you really want, but it might be easier to use some cans of food, or a heavy mortar if you have one.

Vegetable oil, for griddling
1 tsp smoked paprika
1 tsp garlic salt
1 tsp dried thyme
1 tsp freshly ground
  black pepper
1 small spatchcocked chicken
  (about 1kg/2lb 4oz)
  or two poussin

For the green goddess dressing
½ avocado
1 tsp Dijon mustard
3 tbsp buttermilk
1 tsp cider vinegar
Sea salt
3 tbsp olive oil or avocado oil

To serve
Mixed salad leaves
Small handful of tarragon
  leaves
½ avocado
2 thick slices of sourdough
  bread
75g (3oz) Gorgonzola or
  soft blue cheese

1. Place a griddle (grill) pan over a high heat until smoking hot, then brush it with oil.

2. Mix together the smoked paprika, garlic salt, thyme and black pepper, then sprinkle all over the chicken.

3. Put the chicken, skin-side down, on the hot griddle, place a heavy baking tray on top and weigh it down with a few heavy cans. Allow to cook for 5 minutes, then turn the bird over and cook for a further 5 minutes.

4. While the chicken is cooking, make the dressing: put all the ingredients for it into a small blender with 3 tablespoons water and blitz until smooth.

5. Put the salad leaves into a bowl with the tarragon leaves. Slice the avocado and add that too.

6. Remove the chicken from the griddle pan and place on a board to rest. Put the slices of sourdough bread on the griddle and toast for 1–2 minutes in the spiced chicken fat.

7. Tear or cut the bread into croutons and crumble or cube the cheese. Add both to the salad. Drizzle with the dressing and toss to coat. Put any excess dressing into a bowl to serve with the chicken.

8. Cut the chicken into quarters and serve on the board with the salad on the side for people to help themselves.

CHEF'S TIP
Use a heavy upturned frying pan to weigh the chicken down and carefully add half a cup of water to the pan – the steam will help the chicken cook more quickly.

Chicken schnitzel with gherkin crème fraîche

Flattening chicken breasts takes a few seconds, but cuts the cooking time by a good five minutes, and they can then be shallow- rather than deep-fried too. Schnitzel is a real crowd-pleaser, but it will take longer than ten minutes if you double the recipe because you will need to cook the coated chicken in batches. By the way, for my American readers, what we call gherkins in the UK are what you call pickles in the US.

Vegetable oil, for frying
2 small skinless chicken breasts
2 eggs
2 tbsp soy sauce
2 tbsp plain (all-purpose) flour
2 tbsp panko breadcrumbs
1 tsp chopped dill
Freshly ground black pepper
Lemon wedges, to serve

For the gherkin crème fraîche
2 tsp Dijon or French's mustard
2 tbsp crème fraîche
  (sour cream)
2 large gherkins (pickles),
  cut into batons
Pinch of chopped dill
Dash of gherkin pickling liquid
  (optional)

CHEF'S TIP
Once the chicken is coated in breadcrumbs, roll it between two pieces of baking (parchment) paper with a rolling pin to really press the crumbs into the meat and ensure that less fall off while cooking.

IF YOU HAVE MORE TIME...
...use a spoonful of the hot oil to fry two eggs in a frying pan and serve them on top of the schnitzels.

1. Place a large, non-stick frying pan (skillet) over a medium–high heat and pour in a 2cm (¾ inch) depth of oil.

2. Slice the chicken breasts in half horizontally, but not all the way through, and open them out like a book. Season with pepper.

3. Sandwich the opened breasts between two sheets of cling film (plastic wrap) or baking (parchment) paper and bash with a rolling pin or meat hammer until evenly flattened to about 1cm (½ inch) thick.

4. Crack the eggs into a wide, shallow bowl, add the soy sauce and mix together with a fork.

5. Put the flour and the panko breadcrumbs into two separate bowls.

6. Dip the chicken pieces first into the flour, then the beaten eggs, and finally the breadcrumbs, until they are well coated.

7. Add the crumbed chicken to the hot oil and fry for 2–3 minutes on each side.

8. Meanwhile, make the gherkin crème fraîche: mix the mustard and crème fraîche together in a bowl, then stir in the gherkin batons and chopped dill. Loosen the mixture with a dash of the pickling liquid (if required).

9. Using a slotted spoon, remove the chicken from the oil and drain on kitchen paper (paper towel).

10. Serve with a green salad and a generous spoonful of the gherkin crème fraîche.

Cornflake chicken sliders with gochujang mayonnaise

Once you've tried the crunch and flavour of cornflake-coated chicken, you might never go back to breadcrumbs! And to take the crunch factor up to the next level, I dip the buns into a combination of crispy fried onions and roasted peanuts. It looks and tastes great, but you can leave this step out if you are in a hurry. The gochujang (Korean chilli sauce) is also optional, but I really love the kick.

65g (2 cups) cornflakes
2 skinless chicken breasts
3 eggs
4 tbsp plain (all-purpose) flour
Vegetable oil, for frying
½ cucumber
2 spring onions (scallions)
Small handful of coriander
   (cilantro) leaves
2 tbsp fish sauce
Zest and juice of 1 lime
100g (⅔ cup) roasted
   peanuts, crushed (optional)
3 heaped tbsp crispy fried
   onions (optional)
4 brioche burger buns
4 Little Gem lettuce leaves
Sea salt

For the gochujang mayonnaise
2 tbsp gochujang chilli sauce
3 tbsp mayonnaise
Zest and juice of 1 lime

1. Start by making the gochujang mayonnaise: put all the ingredients for it into a bowl and mix together until thoroughly combined. Set aside.

2. Crush the cornflakes in a bowl until they are just bigger than breadcrumbs.

3. Slice the chicken breasts in half horizontally so you have four thin pieces of chicken.

4. Crack the eggs into a wide, shallow bowl and beat with a fork. Put the flour into a similar bowl and season with a little salt. Put the crushed cornflakes into a third bowl. Dip the chicken first into the seasoned flour, then the egg and finally the cornflakes.

5. Place a large frying pan (skillet) over a medium–high heat and pour in a 2cm (¾ inch) depth of oil. When hot, add the chicken pieces and cook for 2 minutes on each side. Drain on kitchen paper (paper towel).

6. Slice the cucumber into ribbons using a speed peeler, and roughly chop the spring onions. Place in a bowl with the coriander leaves, fish sauce, lime zest and juice and toss together.

7. If using the crushed peanuts and crispy fried onions, combine them in a bowl.

8. Split the buns in half and lay them out. Spoon a dollop of the gochujang mayonnaise onto the bottom halves and spread a little on the outside of the tops. Dip the tops into the peanut mixture (if using).

9. Put the lettuce leaves on top of the mayonnaise inside the buns, followed by some of the cucumber salad and the crispy chicken. Put the bun lids on top before serving.

Teriyaki-glazed duck with sticky plums

The combination of duck, teriyaki sauce and sticky plums reminds me of crispy duck pancakes with rich, fruity hoisin sauce, a great favourite in the Ramsay house, but this simple recipe takes a fraction of the time. You can easily double up the recipe if you're feeding more people, but make sure you have a big enough pan to cook four duck breasts at the same time.

2 x 160g (5½oz) duck breasts
2 ripe plums
4 tbsp brown sugar
1 star anise
2 tbsp rice wine vinegar
2 tbsp teriyaki sauce
300g (11oz) pak choi or choi sum (bok choy or choy sum)
Small handful of coriander (cilantro) leaves
Sea salt

IF YOU HAVE MORE TIME...

...serve with soba noodles dressed with toasted sesame oil.

1. Fill the kettle with water and bring to the boil. Place a heavy-based frying pan (skillet) over a high heat.

2. Using a sharp knife, score the skin on the duck breasts. Season with salt and place in the pan, skin-side down. Put a saucepan weighed down with a few heavy cans on top of the duck and cook for 4 minutes.

3. Cut the plums in half, discarding the stones, and place in a small, non-stick frying pan with the sugar and star anise over a medium heat. When the sugar starts to caramelise, add the vinegar and allow to simmer until needed.

4. When the duck has cooked for 4 minutes, flip it over and cook for a further 4 minutes.

5. Quarter the pak choi.

6. Spoon the teriyaki sauce over the duck breasts and remove them from the pan. Allow to rest on a board.

7. Put the pak choi into the frying pan and cook for 2–3 minutes, until soft. Arrange the pak choi and sticky plums on a plate. Slice the duck and place on top, then drizzle with any plum juices and dress with the coriander leaves before serving.

Chicken and butternut squash curry

This is how we do a midweek curry in a hurry at home, especially when the kids are here, there and everywhere. Honestly, it's one of the easiest and quickest curries you will ever make, especially if you grate rather than dice the squash and onion, and cut the chicken into small cubes. I didn't cut the chicken small enough when I cooked this on YouTube and ended up going two minutes over... Tilly said it should be *Ramsay in 12*!

½ butternut squash, preferably the seed-free 'neck' end, peeled
Vegetable oil, for frying
2½ tsp garam masala
1 large red onion
1 chilli, deseeded if you want a milder heat
2.5cm (1 inch) piece of fresh ginger, peeled
2 chicken breasts, diced
50g (⅓ cup) frozen peas
240g (1 cup) canned tomatoes
250ml (1 cup) coconut milk
2 tbsp chicken or vegetable stock
30g (1 cup) fresh spinach
Sea salt and freshly ground black pepper

1. Place a high-sided, non-stick frying pan (skillet) over a medium–high heat.

2. Meanwhile, use the large side of a box grater to coarsely grate the squash.

3. Add a drizzle of oil to the pan, then add the grated squash. Season with salt, then stir in the garam masala.

4. As the squash cooks, peel and grate the onion and add it to pan. Stir well and allow to cook for 1–2 minutes.

5. Meanwhile, roughly chop the chilli and add to the pan, then grate in the ginger and allow to cook for 1–2 minutes.

6. Make a well in the middle of the pan and drizzle in a little oil. Add the diced chicken, season with salt and toss to combine. Cook for 1–2 minutes, then add the peas and cook for a further minute.

7. Add the tomatoes, coconut milk and stock, stir well, then bring to the boil and allow to simmer for 4–5 minutes, until the chicken is cooked.

8. Stir in the spinach and cook until it has wilted. Remove the pan from the heat and serve with rice and roti (see note below), if making.

IF YOU HAVE MORE TIME...
...make roti flatbreads to go with your curry. They need 15 minutes to rest before cooking, so make them before the curry and they will be ready to go when you are. Put 120g (1 cup) plain (all-purpose) flour into a bowl and add a pinch of salt and a glug of olive oil, then pour in 120ml (½ cup) water, stirring with a spatula until a dough forms. At this point, rest the dough for 15 minutes. When the curry is bubbling away, place a large, non-stick frying pan over a high heat and sprinkle with sea salt and a little drizzle of olive oil. Divide the dough into four equal pieces and roll into balls, then roll each ball out until nice and thin. Place in the hot pan one at a time and cook for 1–2 minutes on each side, until slightly charred.

Coconut chicken with sweet peanut dipping sauce

The marinade used here is seriously tasty, as is the dipping sauce, and both are made almost entirely from ingredients you can keep in your cupboards, so they're always on hand if you're looking for a quick fix. They would also work with prawns, pork or cubes of tofu. For a change, you could thread the chicken onto skewers and cook them over a barbecue for extra flavour. Serve with rice, salad or an Asian slaw.

125ml (½ cup) coconut milk
3 tbsp soy sauce
2 tbsp coconut palm sugar,
   or dark brown sugar or honey
85ml (⅓ cup) lime juice
2 tbsp ginger paste
1 tbsp garlic paste
2 tsp curry powder
750g (1½lb) chicken thigh
   or breast fillets, cut into
   2.5cm (1 inch) pieces
Coconut oil, for frying
80g (⅓ cup) smooth
   peanut butter
1 tbsp tamarind paste
   (optional)

To serve
Small handful of soft herbs,
   e.g. basil, mint and coriander
   (cilantro)
Toasted coconut flakes
Chopped salted peanuts
Lime wedges

1. Combine the coconut milk, soy sauce, palm sugar, lime juice, ginger, garlic and curry powder in a jug. Mix well, then pour half the mixture over the chicken in a bowl.

2. Place a griddle (grill) pan over a high heat until smoking hot. Brush the pan with coconut oil, then add the chicken pieces and cook over a high heat for 6–8 minutes, turning occasionally, until caramelised and cooked through.

3. Add the peanut butter and tamarind paste (if using) to the reserved marinade and mix until smooth. If it's too thick, add more lime juice to thin to a dipping sauce consistency.

4. Pile the chicken onto a serving dish and scatter over the herbs, toasted coconut flakes and chopped peanuts. Serve with the dipping sauce and wedges of lime.

SERVES 2

Pink pepper duck with butter beans, cavolo nero and honey and orange sauce

Here we have *duck à l'orange*, but not as you know it, thanks to the pink peppercorns, which give the dish a lovely aromatic heat. You could also use cracked black or Sichuan peppercorns, each bringing their own distinctive flavour. Serve this with a well-dressed green salad to offset the richness of the duck and the sweetness of the sauce.

2 x 160g (5½oz) duck breasts
1 tsp pink peppercorns, crushed
1 garlic clove
100g (4oz) cavolo nero (lacinato kale)
Olive oil, for frying
1 x 400g (15oz) can of butter (lima) beans, drained and rinsed
Sea salt

For the honey and orange sauce
1 tbsp runny honey
3 tbsp orange juice
2 tbsp cider vinegar

1. Place a heavy-based frying pan (skillet) over a high heat.

2. Using a sharp knife, score the skin on the duck breasts. Season with salt and the pink peppercorns and place in the hot pan, skin-side down. Allow to cook for 5 minutes, flip and cook for a further 3 minutes, then turn the heat off.

3. Meanwhile, peel and slice the garlic and chop the cavolo nero into bite-sized pieces, discarding the stalks.

4. Place a non-stick frying pan over a medium heat and coat the bottom with olive oil. When hot, add the garlic and cook until lightly golden. Add the cavolo nero and a splash of water, cover with a lid and steam for 2 minutes.

5. Remove the lid and add the drained butter beans. Season with salt and bring to a simmer until needed.

6. To make the sauce, pour the honey into a small saucepan and bring to the boil over a medium–high heat. When the honey starts to caramelise, add the orange juice and reduce the liquid by half. Add the vinegar and simmer until needed.

7. Remove the duck breasts from the pan and slice with a sharp knife.

8. Divide the beans and cavolo nero between two plates and place the duck on top. Spoon over the warm honey sauce before serving.

Chicken liver baguette

Given that chicken livers are so inexpensive and delicious, I'm always amazed they aren't more popular. For me, where there are livers, there has to be brandy – the combination is a classic of French cuisine for a reason, and I love the sweetness the brandy brings, especially if you use calvados (apple or pear brandy). I also up that sweetness with caramelised onion marmalade, a curiously British condiment that we usually serve with cheese or sausages. It can be bought online in the US.

Olive oil, for frying
50g (2oz) pancetta or
 smoked bacon lardons
200g (7oz) chicken livers,
 cleaned and halved
1 small baguette (French stick)
2 tbsp brandy or calvados
1 tsp Tabasco sauce
1 tbsp Worcestershire sauce
2 tbsp crème fraîche
 (sour cream)
1 ripe pear
100g (4oz) chicory (endive)
 or watercress
2 heaped tbsp caramelised
 onion marmalade or jam
1 tsp chopped chives
Sea salt and freshly ground
 black pepper

For the dressing
1 tsp wholegrain mustard
1 tbsp red wine vinegar
2 tbsp light olive oil

1. Preheat the grill (broiler) to high.

2. First make the salad dressing: combine all the ingredients for it in a small bowl and mix well.

3. Place a large, non-stick frying pan (skillet) over a medium heat and coat the bottom of it with a little olive oil. When hot, add the pancetta or bacon lardons and fry until crisp. Drain on kitchen paper (paper towel) and set aside.

4. Return the pan to the heat and add the chicken livers. Allow to cook for 2 minutes, then turn them over.

5. Slice the baguette in half lengthways and place under the hot grill to toast for 1–2 minutes.

6. Add the brandy to the chicken livers and cook until reduced by half, then add the Tabasco and Worcestershire sauce. Lower the heat, season with salt and pepper, then stir in the crème fraîche and allow to simmer until needed.

7. Cut the pear in half and remove the core, then slice very finely. Place in a bowl with the chicory or watercress and the crisp pancetta, add the dressing and toss well.

8. Spread one half of the baguette evenly with the onion marmalade.

9. Spoon the creamy livers on the other half, sprinkle with the chives and sandwich both halves together. Cut into two equal pieces and serve with the salad on the side.

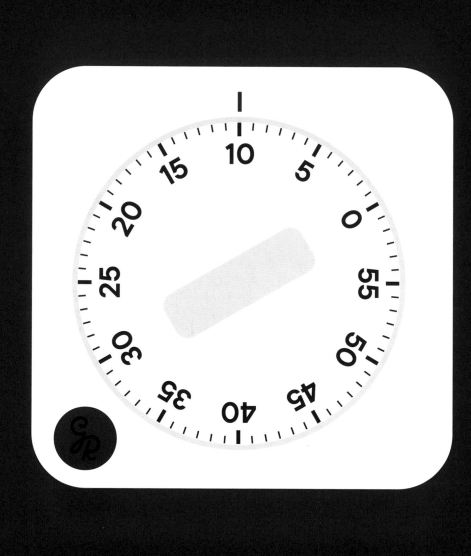

BEEF, LAMB & PORK

Barbecue beef nachos with crispy fried onions

Feeding a crowd isn't that easy in ten minutes, but when ten minutes is all you have, make nachos... loading them up with beef and beans is a bit more work, but it makes them much more substantial. You can double the recipe for a big game or movie night, but it will take longer to put together. Serve with pico de gallo salsa, guacamole and sour cream.

Vegetable oil, for frying
450g (1lb) skirt, hanger
   or flank steak
2 garlic cloves
2 tbsp chipotle chilli paste
1 tbsp fajita spice mix
85ml (⅓ cup) lime juice
125ml (½ cup) IPA or pale ale
120ml (½ cup) barbecue sauce
4 large handfuls of plain
   tortilla chips
1 x 400g (15oz) can of
   mixed beans or black
   beans, drained and rinsed
200g (2 cups) grated Cheddar
   or Monterey Jack cheese
Sea salt and freshly ground
   black pepper

To serve
1 tbsp crispy fried onions
Small handful of coriander
   (cilantro) leaves

1. Preheat the grill (broiler) to high.

2. Place a large frying pan (skillet) over a high heat and coat the bottom of the pan with a thin layer of oil.

3. Slice the steak into thin strips 5mm x 2.5cm (¼ x 1 inch) with a very sharp knife.

4. When the oil is hot, add the steak, season with salt and pepper and cook for 2 minutes, until browned.

5. Peel and crush (mince) the garlic and add it to the pan along with the chipotle paste, fajita spice mix, lime juice and beer and stir to coat. Bring to the boil for 2–3 minutes and allow to reduce by half.

6. Add the barbecue sauce and return to the boil for 1–2 minutes, then remove the pan from the heat.

7. Start building the nachos: put a layer of the tortilla chips in the bottom of an ovenproof baking dish and top with some beans, then some beef and cheese. Repeat layering in this order twice more.

8. Place under the hot grill until the cheese is bubbling. Sprinkle the top with the crispy fried onions and coriander leaves before serving with the optional toppings mentioned in the introduction above if you like.

Treacle-glazed gammon steaks with grilled pineapple and gunpowder potatoes

600g (1lb 5oz) new potatoes, or leftover cooked potatoes

4 x 200g (7oz) thick-cut gammon (ham) steaks or boneless pork loin chops

2 tbsp olive oil or rapeseed (canola) oil, plus extra for frying

4 fresh pineapple fingers or slices

2 tbsp butter

2 tbsp treacle or molasses (see tip)

1 red chilli, deseeded if you want a milder heat, finely sliced

Squeeze of lime or lemon juice

For the gunpowder spice mix

2 tsp black peppercorns

2 tsp pink peppercorns

2 tsp Sichuan peppercorns

2 tsp sea salt

2 tsp mustard seeds

TIP FOR SPEED

When measuring treacle or honey, heat the measuring spoon first under hot running water – you'll find that the sticky stuff will slip straight off the spoon and into your dish. It's more accurate too.

CHEF'S TIP

Snipping into the fat with scissors will help the heat to penetrate the meat, but also gives amazing crispy crackling.

Glazing the gammon steaks with treacle makes them taste like a Christmas ham, but without the rigmarole of boiling and roasting a joint for hours. Make double the spice mix and use it to pep up roast meats, paneer, halloumi or rice. You don't have to serve the grilled pineapple, but I really recommend it. Just not on pizza.

1. Place a griddle (grill) pan or frying pan (skillet) over a high heat. Fill the kettle with water and bring to the boil.

2. If cooking your potatoes from scratch, slice them into rings 5mm (¼ inch) thick and place in a saucepan with just enough boiling water to cover them. Place over a medium–high heat and cook for 6 minutes.

3. Meanwhile, make the gunpowder spice mix by putting all the ingredients for it into a mortar or spice grinder and crushing or blitzing them to a coarse powder.

4. With a sharp knife, remove the rind from the gammon steaks, then use scissors to snip into the fat at 5mm (¼ inch) intervals.

5. When the griddle is smoking hot, drizzle over a little oil and cook the steaks for 3 minutes.

6. Drain the potatoes, then return to the pan on the heat and dry thoroughly, shaking them until they look fluffy.

7. Flip the steaks, then add the pineapple to the pan. Allow to cook for 3 minutes, flipping the pineapple regularly until evenly coloured all over.

8. Place a large, non-stick frying pan over a high heat and add the 2 tablespoons oil followed by the butter. When the butter is bubbling, add the potatoes and cook until golden and crisp. Stir though the gunpowder spice mix, then remove from the heat.

9. Drizzle the treacle or molasses over the steaks, turning them to coat both sides, then remove the pan from the heat.

10. Put the steaks on four plates and place the charred pineapple on top. Sprinkle over some finely sliced chilli and a little lime or lemon juice.

11. Serve with the gunpowder potatoes and a green salad to share.

Mexican cheese and chorizo torta

The word torta means 'sandwich' in Mexico, and I made this chorizo and cheese version on a trip to Tijuana with Gino and Fred. It calls for *bolillos*, which are the soft rolls they use in Mexico, and *queso de Oaxaca*, a firm but stringy mozzarella-style cheese that literally pulls apart in your hands. Both are easy to get hold of in the US, but less so in the UK, where soft half-baguettes and grated mozzarella would be good substitutes.

1 red onion
Olive oil, for frying
300g (11oz) piece of
    chorizo sausage
2 garlic cloves, peeled
1 tsp chilli flakes (optional)
225g (8oz) queso de Oaxaca
    or firm mozzarella cheese
4 small bolillos (soft rolls)
    or small baguettes
    (French sticks)
1 avocado, halved and pitted
Juice of 1 lime
3 romaine lettuce leaves,
    sliced
Large handful of fresh
    coriander (cilantro),
    roughly chopped
1 tbsp pickled red onions,
    from a jar (optional)
1 tbsp sliced jalapeño chillies,
    from a jar (optional)
Sea salt and freshly ground
    black pepper

1. Place a large, non-stick frying pan (skillet) over a medium–high heat.

2. Peel and slice the onion.

3. When the pan is hot, drizzle in a little olive oil, then add the onion. Season with salt and pepper and allow to soften for 1–2 minutes.

4. Chop half of the chorizo into chunks, then peel the remainder and roughly chop or crumble it. Add to the pan and stir well.

5. Crush (mince) or grate the garlic and add to the pan with the chilli flakes (if using) and allow to cook for 2–3 minutes, stirring regularly.

6. If using queso de Oaxaca, peel the layers to shred the cheese; if using mozzarella, chop it into strips or cubes.

7. Slice the rolls open.

8. Mash the avocado on the bottom halves of the bread, then season with lime juice, salt and pepper. Add the lettuce and coriander, followed by the pickled onions and jalapeños (if using) and top with the chorizo and cheese. Put the bread lids on and serve with a crunchy green salad.

Thai meatball lettuce wraps with nam jim dipping sauce

To eat these fragrant lamb meatballs, put a couple of them into a lettuce leaf, add a spoonful of rice and some salad, then wrap everything up and dip it in the sauce – a bit like an Asian burrito! If you have more time, make a double batch of the meatballs useful and freeze half so that you have the makings of a really satisfying meal in the middle of the week.

Zest of 2 limes
1 heaped tbsp Thai green
   curry paste
½ bunch of coriander (cilantro)
500g (1lb 2oz) minced
   (ground) lamb
Vegetable oil, for frying
Sea salt and freshly ground
   black pepper

For the nam jim sauce
60g (generous ⅓ cup)
   roasted peanuts
3 tbsp fish sauce
Juice of 1 lime
1 tsp chilli flakes
2 tbsp maple syrup

To serve
100g (4oz) radishes
½ cucumber
4 spring onions (scallions)
Small handful of mixed
   salad leaves
Small handful of chopped
   chives
500g (1lb 2oz) cooked rice
Leaves of 1 butter (Bibb)
   lettuce or Little Gem
2 limes, halved

1. Zest the limes into a large bowl and add the Thai green curry paste.

2. Roughly chop half the coriander and mix it with the paste.

3. Add the lamb, season with salt and pepper and gently fold through the paste. Divide the mixture into about 10 equal pieces, then roll them into balls. Flatten the balls a little between your palms.

4. Now make the nam jim dipping sauce: roughly chop or crush the peanuts and put them into a bowl with the fish sauce, lime juice, chilli flakes and maple syrup. Stir to combine.

5. Place a large, non-stick frying pan (skillet) over a medium–high heat and add a drizzle of oil. When hot, add the meatballs and cook for 2 minutes on each side.

6. While the meatballs are cooking, slice the radishes, cucumber and spring onions and put them into a bowl with the salad leaves and chives. Toss together.

7. Warm the rice.

8. Remove the meatballs from the pan and season again with salt and pepper.

9. Arrange the meatballs on a large platter with the leaf salad, offering the lettuce leaves and rice separately, along with the dipping sauce and lime halves.

TIP FOR SPEED
When making meatballs or burgers, rub your hands with a little vegetable oil so the mixture won't stick to your fingers. It makes rolling meatballs so much quicker.

Weeping tiger spiced beef salad

This Thai beef salad is on the menu at Lucky Cat, my Asian restaurant in London, and it packs a bit of a punch – which is probably why the tiger is weeping! Or is it because the hunter shot his coveted cow, another explanation for the tears? You can reduce or remove the chilli if you don't like the heat, but the tiger will definitely become more of a pussy cat.

4 x 180–200g (6¼–7oz) beef fillets or sirloin steaks
Vegetable oil, for frying
Large pinch of ground cumin
2 heads of chicory (endive)
¼ red onion
4 tbsp crispy fried onions
4 tbsp puffed brown rice
Small handful of coriander (cilantro) leaves, stalks reserved for the dressing
Small handful of Thai or regular basil leaves
Small handful of mint leaves
1 lime, sliced
Sea salt and freshly ground black pepper

For the dressing
¼ red onion
2 garlic cloves
1 large green chilli, deseeded for a milder heat
2 tbsp fish sauce
Juice of 4 limes
3 tbsp tamarind paste
2 tbsp dark brown sugar
3 tbsp golden (corn) syrup or palm sugar
Coriander stalks (reserved from the salad ingredients)
6 plum tomatoes

1. Place a griddle (grill) pan or frying pan (skillet) over a high heat.

2. Season the beef with salt and pepper. When the pan is smoking hot, add a drizzle of oil and cook the beef for 2–3 minutes on each side, depending on the thickness.

3. Meanwhile, combine all the dressing ingredients, apart from the coriander stalks and tomatoes, in a small blender and blitz for 20–30 seconds.

4. Roughly chop the coriander stalks and cut each tomato into six pieces. Place in a bowl and pour over the dressing.

5. Transfer the beef to a plate, sprinkle over a pinch of ground cumin and set aside to rest.

6. Meanwhile, make the salad: slice the chicory lengthways, cutting the leaves into 3–4 pieces, and put into a salad bowl. Finely slice the onion and add to the bowl along with the crispy fried onions, puffed rice and herbs. Toss to combine, then scatter over the lime slices.

7. Slice the beef and arrange on four plates. Spoon over the tomatoes and dressing and garnish with the salad.

IF YOU HAVE MORE TIME...
...cook the beef on the barbecue. The smoky, charred flavours work really well with the sharp, spicy dressing.

Steak sandwich

A good steak sandwich is unbeatable, and for me, it's at its best when made with a really tasty cut of beef, such as onglet, otherwise known as hanger steak. This less well-known piece is sometimes called the butcher's cut, supposedly because it is so good that the butcher always keeps it for himself! I urge you to wrestle it off your local butcher and try it in this excellent sandwich.

3 tbsp mayonnaise
1 tbsp Dijon mustard
Splash of Tabasco sauce
Vegetable oil, for frying
2 x 120g (4½oz) onglet,
    hanger or rump steaks
4 small Portobello mushrooms
1 red onion
1 tbsp Worcestershire sauce
2–3 sprigs of thyme
Splash of Guinness (optional)
Ciabatta loaf
Small handful of watercress
    or mixed leaves
40g (1½oz) blue cheese, sliced
(optional)
Sea salt and freshly ground
    black pepper

1. Place a griddle (grill) pan over a high heat.

2. Put the mayonnaise into a small bowl and stir through the mustard and Tabasco.

3. When the griddle is smoking hot, brush with a little oil. Season the steaks all over with salt and place on the griddle for 3 minutes.

4. Discard the mushroom stalks, then place the caps on the griddle pan beside the steak. Allow to cook for 4 minutes, turning occasionally.

5. Peel the onion, slice into rings 5mm (¼ inch) thick and place on the griddle to fry.

6. Flip the steaks and cook for a further 3 minutes. Preheat the grill (broiler) to high.

7. When the onion is cooked, transfer it to a small bowl and dress with the Worcestershire sauce. Put a plate on top of the bowl so they keep cooking.

8. Roughly chop the thyme on a board and place the steaks on top to rest.

9. Deglaze the griddle with the Guinness (if using) and add this liquid and the mushrooms to the onions. Stir to combine.

10. Meanwhile, slice the ciabatta in half lengthways and place under the grill to toast.

11. Once toasted, spread each side with the mustard mayonnaise.

12. Roll the steak in the thyme and season with pepper. Slice and place on one side of the bread, then spoon over the mushrooms and onions. Top with the watercress, blue cheese (if using) and the other piece of bread and slice in half before serving.

Balsamic lamb chops with tomato salad and anchovy dressing

Sometimes feeding a family can feel like Groundhog Day, especially in recent times, when we've all been stuck at home because of the pandemic. I find it helpful to have a few recipes up my sleeve that use familiar ingredients but with a different sauce, rub or dressing to shake things up. Putting the hot lamb chops into the balsamic vinegar creates an instant sweet-and-sour marinade that goes really well with the punchy anchovy-dressed tomatoes.

1 garlic clove
2 tbsp balsamic vinegar
Pinch of chilli flakes
½ small handful of mint leaves
8 lamb chops
Vegetable oil, for frying
1 banana shallot (echalion) or
    2 regular shallots
1 heaped tbsp small capers
200g (7oz) golden and red
    cherry tomatoes on the vine
Small handful of flat-leaf
    parsley leaves
2 Little Gem lettuces or
    heads of radicchio, separated
Sea salt

For the anchovy dressing
6 tbsp mayonnaise
3 tsp Gentleman's Relish,
    or 4 anchovy fillets, chopped
    and mixed to a paste
1½ tbsp red wine vinegar
Freshly ground black pepper

1. Place a griddle (grill) pan or frying pan (skillet) over a high heat.

2. Peel the garlic, then crush (mince) or grate it into a large bowl. Add the balsamic vinegar, chilli flakes and mint leaves. Set aside until needed.

3. Season the chops with salt on both sides.

4. When the griddle is smoking hot, drizzle over a little oil and cook the chops for 2 minutes.

5. Peel and slice the shallot into rings 5mm (¼ inch) thick and place in a salad bowl with the capers.

6. Flip the chops and cook for a further 2 minutes.

7. Slice the tomatoes and add them to the shallots along with the parsley and the separated lettuce or radicchio leaves.

8. When the chops are cooked, transfer them to the bowl with the balsamic, chilli flakes and mint. Stir to coat and leave to rest.

9. To make the dressing, put the mayonnaise and Gentleman's Relish or anchovy paste into a bowl, add the red wine vinegar, season with pepper and whisk together until fully combined.

10. Pour the anchovy dressing over the salad and toss to coat.

11. Put the chops on plates and drizzle over a little of their balsamic dressing. Serve with the salad on the side.

Sausages and mash with caramelised onion gravy

3–4 peeled potatoes
2 tbsp olive oil, plus extra
for frying
4–6 pork sausages
2 garlic cloves
2 sprigs of rosemary
1 red onion
2 tbsp butter, plus 3 tsp
for the onions
1 tsp sugar
2 tbsp balsamic vinegar
2 tsp Worcestershire sauce
3–4 tbsp beef, chicken
or vegetable stock
Pinch of smoked salt
1–2 tsp wholegrain mustard
(optional)
1 tbsp chopped chives
(optional)
Sea salt

CHEF'S TIPS

When you take the frying
pan out of the oven, leave
a tea towel folded around
the handle to prevent you
from burning your hand if
you forget that it's hot.

Mashing the potatoes over
the heat will make them
extra fluffy and lump-free.

IF YOU HAVE MORE TIME...

...sauté chard to serve
alongside your sausages
and mash.

You really can cook bangers and mash from scratch in ten minutes. If you don't believe me, look at my YouTube video: not only do I pull it off in 10 minutes and 57 seconds (the 57 seconds was for plating), but the result is amazing. I use red onions for the gravy because they are sweet and less acidic than white.

1. Preheat the oven to 160°C/140°C fan/325°F/Gas 3. Fill the kettle with water and bring to the boil, then use to half-fill a saucepan and return to the boil over a medium–high heat.

2. Finely dice the potatoes and add them to the boiling water. The water should just cover them, so tip away any excess. Cover with a lid and cook for 5 minutes, until tender.

3. Place an ovenproof frying pan (skillet) over a medium heat. Drizzle a little olive oil into the pan, add the sausages and increase the heat to medium–high.

4. Peel the garlic, then flatten it with the side of a large knife. Add to the pan with the rosemary sprigs and cook for 2–3 minutes, until the sausages begin to colour.

5. Meanwhile, place a non-stick frying pan over a medium–high heat, then peel and finely slice the onion. Add a drizzle of olive oil to the pan, add the onion and cook for 1–2 minutes, stirring regularly.

6. When the sausages are beginning to colour, add the 2 tablespoons butter. When melted, baste the sausages with the butter and garlic. Place the frying pan in the oven for 6–7 minutes.

7. Sprinkle the sugar over the onions, season with salt and add 2 teaspoons of the butter. When the butter has melted, add the balsamic vinegar and Worcestershire sauce and allow to reduce for 1–2 minutes.

8. Add enough stock to cover the onions, bring to the boil and reduce for 3 minutes.

9. Once the potatoes are cooked, drain and return them to the saucepan. Mash with a potato masher over the heat, then add the olive oil and stir thoroughly. Reduce the heat and mix in the smoked salt, mustard and chives (if using). Set aside.

10. Add the remaining teaspoon of butter to the onions and stir through as it melts.

11. Divide the mashed potatoes between two plates. Place the sausages on top of the mash, then drizzle over the onion gravy before serving.

Tandoori lamb steaks with black lentils and charred broccoli

Curry paste is an amazing shortcut when you don't have much time. Just mix this tandoori paste with yoghurt and smear it over the lamb to add intense flavour with minimal effort. You could also use it on lamb chops, or a butterflied leg if you have more time. Taking a couple of minutes to marinate the lamb the night before will make this dish even tastier.

2 tbsp tandoori paste
3 tbsp natural (plain) yoghurt
2 x 225g (8oz) lamb steaks
Vegetable oil, for frying
1 x 250g (9oz) packet of
  cooked beluga lentils
200g (7oz) Tenderstem
  broccoli
1 tbsp roughly chopped
  mint leaves
Juice of 1 lime
1 tbsp flat-leaf parsley leaves

IF YOU HAVE MORE TIME...
...start marinating the lamb the night before. It will penetrate more deeply and be extra delicious.

1. Place a griddle (grill) pan or frying pan (skillet) over a high heat.

2. Put the tandoori paste and 1 tablespoon of the yoghurt into a large bowl and mix well. Add the lamb steaks and stir to coat the meat.

3. When the griddle or frying pan is smoking hot, drizzle over a little oil and cook the lamb for 3 minutes.

4. Warm the lentils according to the packet instructions.

5. Flip the steaks and cook for a further 3 minutes.

6. Transfer the steaks to a plate, then put the broccoli into the empty pan and cook for 2–3 minutes, flipping regularly until tender.

7. Fold the remaining yoghurt and the chopped mint through the lentils and divide between two plates. Slice the lamb and place on top of the lentils. Pour over any juices from the plate over the top, then squeeze over the lime juice.

8. Scatter with the parsley leaves and serve with warm chapattis or naan bread.

SERVES 2

Bacon cheeseburger with sriracha mayonnaise

From raw ingredients to an incredible juicy burger in just ten minutes... this is my quickest burger ever! Remember that the thicker you make the patties, the longer they will take to cook, so if you want these on the table in under ten, press your burgers until they are a little thinner for a quicker cooking time. Replace the sriracha with wholegrain, English or Dijon mustard if chilli isn't your thing.

225g (8oz) minced
  (ground) beef
1 egg yolk
½ frozen red chilli, deseeded
  if you want a milder heat
Vegetable oil, for frying
4 thick slices of onion
4 rashers (slices) of bacon
2 brioche burger buns
1 tsp butter
2 slices of Cheddar cheese
2 Little Gem lettuce leaves
2–4 tomato slices
Sea salt and freshly ground
  black pepper

For the sriracha mayonnaise
2 tbsp mayonnaise
1 tsp sriracha (or more
  if you like it hotter)

CHEF'S TIP
Put a handful of chillies into the freezer and grate a little as and when needed into curries, sauces and burgers. Freezing the chilli makes it really easy to grate with minimum fuss.

1. Preheat the grill (broiler) to high. Place a griddle (grill) pan or frying pan (skillet) over a medium–high heat.

2. Season the beef with salt and pepper. Add the egg yolk, then grate in the chilli and mix together with clean hands. Divide the beef in half and form into two patties about 2.5cm (1 inch) thick.

3. Drizzle the hot pan with oil. Put the burgers in it and season with salt and pepper. Allow to cook for 3–4 minutes.

4. Put the onion slices and bacon in the pan and increase the heat to high.

5. Meanwhile, combine the sriracha mayonnaise ingredients in a bowl, season with salt and pepper and stir to combine.

6. Flip the burgers, bacon and onions and continue to cook for 4–5 minutes.

7. Toast the buns, cut-side up, under the hot grill for 1–2 minutes.

8. Add the butter to the griddle, then place a slice of cheese on top of each burger. Cover with a lid or upturned saucepan, or place under the hot grill, until the cheese has melted.

9. When the bacon and onions are cooked, drain them on kitchen paper (paper towel).

10. Put the bottom halves of the buns on two plates, spread with the sriracha mayonnaise and add a lettuce leaf and tomato slices to each one. Follow with some of the onion slices, the burgers, bacon, a little more mayonnaise, more onion slices and finish with the lids.

Lamb chops with smoked chipotle vinaigrette, creamy mashed peas and caramelised potatoes

This isn't just meat and two veg... this is chargrilled lamb chops with crisp potatoes, sautéd mushrooms and crushed peas, drizzled with a smoky vinaigrette. Here's more proof that amazing food doesn't always take lots of time or effort.

Vegetable oil, for frying
6 small lamb chops
3 garlic cloves
4 small mushrooms, e.g. button, chestnut or cremini
225g (8oz) cooked new potatoes, or leftover cooked potatoes
½ small red onion
2 tbsp butter
2 spring onions (scallions)
Sea salt and freshly ground black pepper

For the creamy mashed peas
150g (1 cup) frozen peas
1 tsp butter
½ tbsp crème fraîche (sour cream)
Zest of ½ lemon

For the chipotle vinaigrette
2 tsp wholegrain mustard
1 tbsp apple cider vinegar
3 tbsp olive oil
1 chipotle chilli paste

1. Place a griddle (grill) pan or frying pan (skillet) over a high heat.

2. Drizzle a little vegetable oil over the lamb chops and season with salt and pepper. When the griddle pan is smoking hot, add the chops and cook for 1–2 minutes.

3. Peel the garlic cloves, flatten 2 of them with the blade of a large knife and add to the pan. Cut the mushrooms into quarters, add them to the same pan and continue to cook for 1–2 minutes.

4. Place a large, non-stick frying pan over a medium–high heat and coat the bottom of it with a layer of oil. While the oil is heating, cut the potatoes in half, then add to the hot oil and cook for 1–2 minutes.

5. Meanwhile, peel and slice the onion, then add to the potatoes. Flatten the remaining garlic clove, add it to the pan and season with salt and pepper. Toss and continue to cook for 2–3 minutes. Add 1 tablespoon of the butter and allow to bubble.

6. To make the creamy mashed peas, fill the kettle with water and bring to the boil. Pour it into a saucepan, bring back to the boil, then add the peas. Cover with a lid and cook for 2–3 minutes.

7. Flip the chops, add the remaining butter and continue to cook for 2 minutes. Meanwhile, make the chipotle vinaigrette: put all the ingredients into a jar and shake well until emulsified. Season with salt and pepper. Drizzle a little over the chops, then remove the pan from the heat.

8. Trim and slice the spring onions and toss them through the potato mixture before removing the pan from the heat.

9. Drain the peas and return them to the saucepan. Add the butter and crème fraîche, season with salt and pepper, then crush together with a potato masher. Grate in the lemon zest and stir through.

10. Arrange the chops on two plates with the mushrooms, potatoes and a spoonful of peas. Drizzle over a little of the chipotle vinaigrette before serving.

Pork tenderloin with grilled corn salsa and crispy prosciutto

The combination of charred sweetcorn with pan-fried pork loin and heritage (heirloom) tomatoes is incredible. You can use canned corn if you are in a hurry, but grilling the cobs will give the salsa much more flavour, so it's definitely worth the effort and extra time. You don't have to add the prosciutto, but its crisp texture and saltiness finish the dish beautifully.

450g (1lb) pork tenderloin, cut into 8 medallions
1 tbsp garlic powder
1 tbsp freshly ground black pepper
2 corn on the cob
Vegetable oil, for frying
1 red onion
2 tbsp red wine vinegar
1 tsp chopped chilli, from a jar
250g (9oz) heritage (heirloom) tomatoes
2 large handfuls of baby spinach
Small handful of Greek or regular basil
8 prosciutto slices
2 tbsp butter
Sea salt

1. Place two griddle (grill) pans or frying pans (skillets) over a high heat.

2. Season the pork medallions all over with the garlic powder, black pepper and some sea salt.

3. When the pans are hot, brush the corn with a little oil, place in one of the pans and cook for 6–8 minutes, turning regularly, until charred all over.

4. Drizzle some oil into the second pan, add the medallions and allow to cook for 3 minutes.

5. Peel and finely slice the onion and put it into a bowl with the vinegar and chopped chilli.

6. Flip the medallions and cook for a further 2 minutes.

7. Slice, halve or quarter the tomatoes, depending on their size, add them to the onions.

8. Remove the corn cobs from the pan and shave the kernels from the husks. Add them to the tomato mixture, along with the spinach and basil, then season with salt and toss together.

9. Lay the prosciutto slices in the empty pan and allow to crisp for 30–60 seconds on each side.

10. Transfer the medallions to a board to rest.

11. Add the butter to the prosciutto pan and remove from the heat.

12. Arrange the medallions on a serving dish and place the crispy prosciutto on top. Drizzle over the melted butter from the pan and serve with the corn salsa.

Blackened steak with kimchi fried rice and pickled radish

Bavette steak, or flank steak as it is known in America, comes from a well-used part of the cow, so has quite a different texture from more premium steak cuts, such as ribeye and sirloin. Since it has more connective tissue (and therefore more flavour), it needs to be cooked quickly over a high heat, as here, or braised much more slowly at a lower temperature. When slicing it, always remember to cut across the grain to maximise tenderness.

1 tbsp hoisin sauce
1 tbsp soy sauce or tamari
2 x 175g (6oz) bavette (flank) steaks
Vegetable oil, for frying
140g (scant 1 cup) kimchi, from a jar, plus 1 tbsp of the juice
250g (1⅓ cups) cooked jasmine or basmati rice
2 spring onions (scallions)
2 eggs
6 breakfast radishes or 5cm (2 inch) piece of daikon radish
2 tbsp black sesame seeds or nigella seeds
1 tsp chopped chilli, from a jar
Sea salt and freshly ground black pepper

1. Place a griddle (grill) pan or frying pan (skillet) over a high heat.

2. Put the hoisin and soy sauce into a bowl and mix together. Add the steak and stir to coat.

3. When the griddle or frying pan is smoking hot, drizzle over a little oil and cook the steaks for 2–3 minutes.

4. Meanwhile, place a large, non-stick frying pan over a medium heat and add a little oil. While the oil is heating, roughly chop the kimchi, then add it to the pan. Add the rice and stir to combine.

5. Slice the spring onions, reserving the green tops for serving, and add to the pan with the rice and kimchi.

6. Flip the steaks over and cook for a further 2–3 minutes.

7. Place a second non-stick frying pan over a medium heat and add a little oil. When hot, crack in the eggs and fry for 2 minutes, until the whites are firm and beginning to crisp around the edges.

8. Finely grate the radishes into a bowl. Season with salt, then stir in the kimchi juice.

9. Divide the hot rice between two bowls. Put a fried egg on top and sprinkle with the sesame seeds, followed by salt and pepper. Finely slice the steaks across the grain and place alongside the rice.

10. Sprinkle over the chopped chilli and reserved spring onion greens before serving with the radish salad on the side.

Za'atar-spiced lamb burgers with harissa yoghurt and preserved lemon

Lamb mince is perfect for burgers because it's naturally fatty and therefore holds together without needing to add an egg to bind it. Adding za'atar – a Middle Eastern mix of dried thyme or oregano, sesame seeds and sumac – gives the patties a beautiful flavour that works really well with the red peppers and harissa yoghurt. The preserved lemons are the icing on the cake, but can be left out if you can't get hold of them or don't love them.

600g (1lb 5oz) minced (ground) lamb
2 heaped tbsp za'atar
Vegetable oil, for frying
1 small red onion
1 small preserved lemon
Small handful of coriander (cilantro) leaves
Juice of ½ lemon
3 tbsp natural (plain) yoghurt
1 heaped tbsp harissa paste
240g (8½oz) roasted (bell) peppers, from a jar
4 burger buns
½ butter (Bibb) lettuce
Sea salt and freshly ground black pepper

1. Place a large, non-stick frying pan (skillet) over a high heat.

2. Put the lamb into a bowl and add the za'atar, season with salt and pepper and mix together with clean hands. Divide into four equal pieces, roll into balls and gently press into thick patties.

3. When the pan is smoking hot, drizzle with a little oil and cook the burgers for 4 minutes.

4. Meanwhile, peel the onion and slice very finely with a mandoline or the blade side of a box grater and put into a bowl.

5. Chop the preserved lemon into quarters, then scoop out and discard the bitter flesh. Finely chop the peel and add to the onions.

6. Add the coriander leaves, squeeze the lemon juice over the top, then toss to combine.

7. Flip the burgers and cook for a further 4 minutes.

8. Put the yoghurt into a small bowl and stir in the harissa paste.

9. Cut the peppers into strips, lay them over the lamb burgers, then remove the pan from the heat.

10. Slice the burger buns in half and spread the 'lids' with half the harissa yoghurt.

11. Shred the lettuce, stir it into the remaining harissa yoghurt and spoon the mixture onto the bottom halves of the buns.

12. Put the burgers on top of the dressed lettuce, then spoon over the onion mixture and cover with the bun lids. Serve with chips (fries) or potato wedges.

Minced beef stir-fry with fried rice

This is a very straightforward stir-fry and can be made with any minced (ground) meat you happen to have in the fridge – beef, turkey, chicken or lamb. And feel free to change any of the veg too – use whatever you like or have available. The trick here is to get the pan really hot before you start, and to break up the meat with your fingers rather than adding it in a great lump, which would cool the pan down and stop the meat from browning.

225g (8oz) minced (ground) beef
Vegetable oil, for frying
1 red chilli
2.5cm (1 inch) piece of fresh ginger, peeled
1 garlic clove, peeled
2 red or yellow (bell) peppers
35g (½ cup) mangetout (snow peas)
1 head of pak choi (bok choy)
2 large white mushrooms
1 tbsp soy sauce
2 tsp fish sauce (optional)
Coriander (cilantro) leaves
Sea salt

For the fried rice
1 large egg, beaten (optional)
165g (1 cup) cold cooked rice
2 spring onions (scallions)

TIP FOR SPEED

To prep a (bell) pepper really quickly, cut off the stalk and stand the pepper on its cut end. Slice around it from top to bottom 3–4 times, leaving behind the white membranes and seeds, and giving you three or four pieces of pepper to use as required.

1. Place a large, non-stick frying pan (skillet) or wok over a medium–high heat.

2. With clean hands, break the beef into smaller pieces and season with salt.

3. Drizzle a little oil into the pan or wok. Once the oil is hot, add the beef, making sure to spread it around the pan.

4. Deseed and finely slice the chilli and add it to the pan. Grate the ginger and garlic directly into the pan and stir well. Increase the heat to high and allow to cook for 1–2 minutes, until the beef is browned and crisp. Transfer to a plate to rest.

5. Slice the peppers (see tip) and add them to the pan. Season with salt, add a drizzle of oil and toss to combine.

6. Slice the mangetout in half lengthways and add them to the pan. Cut the stems from the pak choi and finely slice them. Roll up the leaves and finely slice them too. Add the stems to the pan and toss for about 10 seconds, then add the leaves and toss again.

7. Slice the mushrooms and add them to the pan, followed by the soy sauce and fish sauce (if using). Toss vigorously a few times, then continue to cook for about 30 seconds. Once the mushrooms are tender, transfer the mixture to a second plate and set aside.

8. If making the fried rice, drizzle a little oil into the hot pan and add the beaten egg. Move it quickly around with a spatula, as it cooks in just 10 seconds, then season with salt and add the rice, breaking it up as you stir it into the egg. Transfer to a bowl and set aside, keeping warm until serving.

9. Roughly chop the spring onions and add them to the pan. Toss to combine, then add the plates of vegetables and beef and mix well.

10. Sprinkle with the coriander leaves before dividing between two plates and serving.

SERVES 2

GF

Sirloin steak with sautéd potatoes and chimichurri sauce

2 x 180g–200g (6¼–7oz)
sirloin steaks, brought to
room temperature
Olive oil, for frying
1 sprig of rosemary
6 whole mushrooms
2 stems of cherry tomatoes
on the vine
10–12 cooked new potatoes,
sliced
1½ garlic cloves
2 tsp butter
1 red onion (optional)
4 spring onions (scallions)
Small handful of parsley
Sea salt and freshly ground
black pepper

For the chimichurri sauce
1½ garlic cloves, peeled
and crushed (minced)
Small handful of mint
Small handful of parsley
Small handful of basil
1 red chilli, deseeded if
you want a milder heat
2–3 tbsp olive oil
1 tbsp red wine vinegar
1 tbsp honey
Zest and juice of ½ lemon

If you want to cook meat in a hurry, look no further than steak – it takes literally five minutes for medium-rare, and not much longer if, heaven forbid, you like it more well done. Chimichurri is a salsa from Argentina, and what Argentinians don't know about steak isn't worth knowing, so you can trust that this will be an incredible combination. The sautéd potatoes will only be ready in the time if they are already cooked when you start.

1. Place a griddle (grill) pan or large frying pan (skillet) over a high heat.

2. Smear the steaks with olive oil, then season with salt and pepper. When the pan is smoking hot, drizzle with a little oil and place the steaks in it, followed by the rosemary, mushrooms and tomatoes (still whole and on the vine) and cook for 2–3 minutes.

3. Place a large, non-stick frying pan over a medium–high heat and add a tablespoon of olive oil. Add the potatoes and season with salt and pepper.

4. Flip the mushrooms when browned on one side and continue to cook.

5. Meanwhile, peel the garlic and crush (mince) or grate it into the potatoes. Add a teaspoon of the butter and toss. Peel and finely slice the onion (if using) and add to the pan. Allow to cook for 6–7 minutes, tossing the mixture regularly.

6. Flip the steaks and the mushrooms, then add the remaining teaspoon of butter to the mushrooms. Continue to cook for 2–3 minutes, until caramelised.

7. Meanwhile, place all the chimichurri ingredients, except the lemon zest and juice, in a blender and blitz to a coarse paste.

8. When the steaks are cooked to your liking, turn the heat off under the pan.

9. Trim and chop the spring onions, adding the green parts to the potatoes and the white parts to the chimichurri. Add a little more olive oil to loosen the sauce, if necessary, and finish with the lemon zest and juice.

10. Toss the potatoes and remove from the heat when crisp.

11. Spoon a generous layer of the chimichurri sauce on top of the steaks as they rest.

12. Roughly chop the parsley and stir through the potatoes. Divide between two plates and add the steaks, mushrooms and tomatoes, and drizzle with a little more chimichurri before serving.

CHEF'S TIP
Always dry meat and fish thoroughly with kitchen paper (paper towel) before frying, as any moisture will stop it colouring quickly, increasing the risk of overcooking and reducing the flavour in the final dish.

Harissa lamb neck with herby couscous and courgette salad

Neck of lamb is one of those cuts that should either be cooked quickly over a high heat, like steak, or braised really slowly, like lamb shanks. Given the time frame, these neck fillets are griddled on a smoking-hot pan and served pink in the middle. The combination of the fragrant harissa and sweet pomegranate molasses is beautiful, just what you need to up the ante for a week-night dinner.

4 x 150g (5oz) lamb neck fillets
4 tbsp harissa paste
150g (5oz) couscous
150ml (generous ½ cup) boiling
   vegetable stock or water
Vegetable oil, for frying
1 tsp coriander seeds
1 tsp cumin seeds
1 large courgette (zucchini)
   or 2 small ones
1 tbsp olive oil
1 tsp sumac
4 tbsp natural (plain) yoghurt
2 tbsp pomegranate molasses
Small handful of mint leaves
Small handful of roughly
   chopped dill
2 tbsp pomegranate seeds
Sea salt and freshly ground
   black pepper

1. Place a griddle (grill) pan or frying pan (skillet) over a high heat.

2. Put the lamb neck fillets into a bowl, add the harissa paste and toss to coat the meat.

3. Fill the kettle with water and bring to the boil.

4. Put the couscous into a heatproof bowl and pour over the boiling stock or water. Stir and cover the bowl tightly with cling film (plastic wrap). Set aside for 5 minutes.

5. When the griddle or frying pan is smoking hot, drizzle with vegetable oil and cook the lamb fillets for 4 minutes.

6. Meanwhile, put the coriander and cumin seeds into a mortar and crush until the seeds are cracked.

7. Use a speed peeler to slice the courgette(s) into ribbons, then drizzle with the olive oil and sprinkle over the cracked seeds and the sumac. Add the yoghurt and mix well.

8. Flip the lamb fillets and continue to cook for a further 4 minutes.

9. Pour the pomegranate molasses into a mixing bowl and add the cooked lamb.

10. Stir half the herbs through the couscous with a fork, season with salt and pepper and divide between two plates.

11. Slice the lamb and place on the couscous, pouring any juices over the top. Sprinkle over the pomegranate seeds and the remaining herbs and serve with the courgette and yoghurt salad.

Pan-fried veal chops with Boston baked beans

Traditionally, Boston beans are baked in the oven for hours and hours, but I've pressed the fast-forward button here by using pre-cooked beans, and they can be ready in less than ten minutes. If you have more time, cook them in advance, or double the recipe for the most incredible beans on toast the next day. They would also work with sausages, pork chops or roast pork belly.

Vegetable oil, for frying
2 x 250–300g (9–11oz)
   veal chops
2 tbsp butter
1 tbsp chopped chives
Sea salt and freshly ground
   black pepper

For the Boston beans
2 tbsp olive oil
1 large shallot
2 garlic cloves
1 tsp cumin seeds
1 tsp tomato purée (paste)
1 tsp smoked paprika
120g (4½oz) wood-roasted
   (bell) peppers, from a jar
1 tsp chipotle paste
1 tbsp black treacle (molasses)
1 x 400g (15oz) can of
   butter (lima) beans,
   drained and rinsed
250g (1 cup) tomato passata
   (purée)
Zest and juice of 1 lemon
½ bunch of flat-leaf parsley,
   finely chopped

1. Place a griddle (grill) pan or frying pan (skillet) over a high heat and drizzle with a little vegetable oil.

2. Season the chops with salt, place them in the pan and cook for 4 minutes on each side.

3. Meanwhile, start making the beans: place a heavy-based saucepan over a medium heat and add the olive oil.

4. While the oil is heating, peel and grate the shallot and garlic, then add them to the pan. Season with salt and pepper and cook for 1–2 minutes, until soft.

5. Add the cumin seeds and toast for 1 minute, then add the tomato purée, paprika, roasted peppers, chipotle paste and black treacle. Mix well and allow to cook for 1 minute.

6. Add the beans and passata, stir well and bring to a simmer until needed.

7. When the chops are cooked, use tongs to turn them onto their fatty edge for 60–90 seconds so that it can crisp up. Transfer to a plate and set aside to rest.

8. Add the butter to the empty pan and cook until it turns brown and begins to smell nutty. Stir in the chives and remove from the heat.

9. Season the beans with the lemon zest and juice, salt and pepper and chopped parsley and stir well.

10. Place the chops on two plates, drizzle over the brown butter and serve with a generous spoonful of the beans.

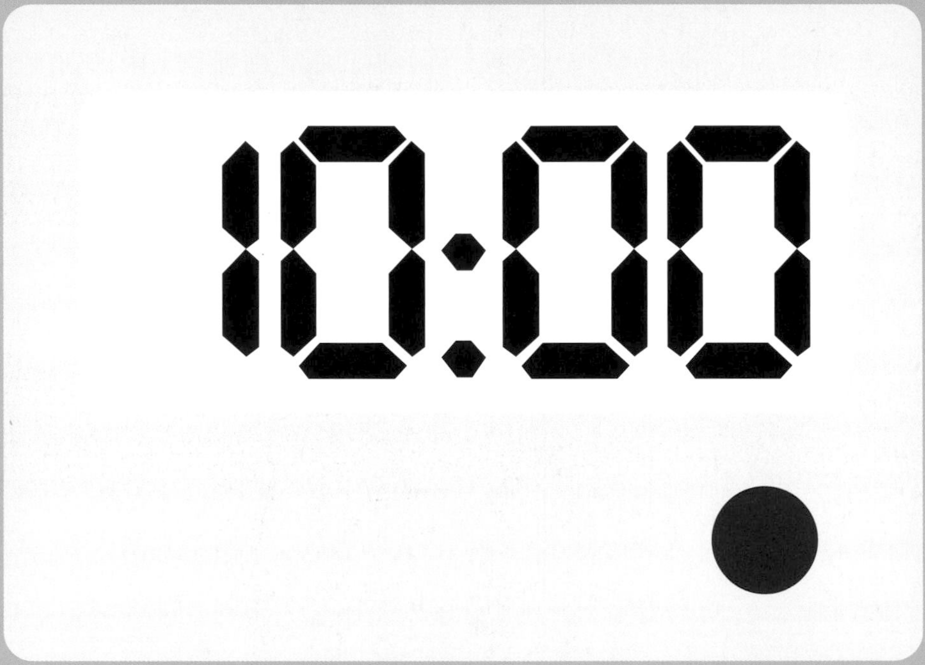
10:00

FISH & SEAFOOD

Salmon ceviche with orange and fennel salad

Ceviche is the ultimate fast food – you don't even need to cook it! Make sure you buy the freshest sushi-grade salmon possible (this means it has been prepared and frozen in a way that makes it safe to eat raw) and let the acid from the lemon juice work its magic. You can swap the salmon for firm-fleshed white fish, such as sea bass or bream, and get creative with the salad, depending on what you have in the fridge.

¼ red onion

½ red chilli

1 lemon

1 blood orange, regular orange or grapefruit

2 baby fennel bulbs, fronds reserved

60g (2 cups) mixed lettuce leaves, e.g. watercress, rocket (arugula), romaine

½ avocado

Olive oil, for dressing

Pinch of sea salt

180g (6¼oz) sushi-grade salmon or sea trout

Pinch of crushed pink peppercorns

1. Start by peeling and finely dicing or grating the onion, then deseed and grate the chilli (see tip).

2. Zest and juice the lemon and mix with the chilli and onion.

3. Peel the orange or grapefruit, removing as much of the pith as you can, then trim off the top and bottom. Cut the remainder widthways into 6 round slices. Squeeze the juice from end offcuts into the onion mixture.

4. Using a mandoline or sharp knife, finely slice the fennel, then mix it with the lettuce leaves and orange slices in a large bowl. Cut the avocado flesh into cubes, then add to the salad and dress with a drizzle of olive oil and a pinch of salt. Toss to combine.

5. Place the fish on a clean board, and, using a very sharp knife, cut into slices 5mm (¼ inch) thick. Lay the slices on a serving dish and spoon over the onion mixture. Gently mix together, then sprinkle with the pink peppercorns and any reserved fennel fronds, roughly chopped. Serve with the salad on the side.

TIP FOR SPEED

To deseed a chilli fast, simply cut off the stalk end, then roll the chilli between your palms over a board or bin. The seeds should simply fall out, leaving you with just the flesh.

Grilled salmon niçoise with brown butter and caper dressing

It turns out that many of the things we think are essential elements of a traditional salad niçoise – tuna, potatoes, green beans – aren't actually traditional at all, so why not swap the tuna for salmon? You can leave out the potatoes and green beans too, if you like, but there must be ripe tomatoes, anchovies and black olives for the true taste of the French Riviera.

400g (14oz) new potatoes
4 eggs
160g (5½oz) green beans, trimmed
1 x 400g (14oz) piece of salmon, or 4 fillets
Vegetable oil, for frying
100g (3 cups) mixed lettuce leaves
150g (5oz) cherry tomatoes, halved
40g (scant ¼ cup) pitted black olives
1 tbsp basil leaves
Sea salt and freshly ground black pepper

For the brown butter and caper dressing
80g (generous ⅓ cup) butter
4 anchovies in oil
2 tbsp fine capers
Zest and juice of 1 lemon
Pinch of chilli flakes
100ml (scant ½ cup) olive oil

1. Place a griddle (grill) pan over a high heat. Fill the kettle with water and bring to the boil.

2. Slice the potatoes into rings 5mm (¼ inch) thick, place them in a saucepan and cover with boiling water. Add the eggs, place over a medium-high heat and cook for 5 minutes.

3. Put the green beans into a steamer and place over the potatoes with the lid on.

4. Meanwhile, season the salmon with sea salt.

5. Drizzle a little oil onto the hot griddle pan and add the fish, skin-side down. Allow to cook for 3 minutes, then flip and cook for a further 3 minutes.

6. While the potatoes, eggs and salmon are cooking, make the dressing: put the butter into a small saucepan and place over a medium heat to melt. Chop the anchovies and crush to make a paste.

7. When the butter is foaming and beginning to smell nutty, add the capers and anchovies. Stir well, then add the lemon zest and juice, chilli flakes and olive oil and stir again. Transfer to a large bowl.

8. Put the mixed leaves and tomatoes into a serving bowl and season with salt and pepper.

9. Remove the beans from the steamer and dry on kitchen paper (paper towel). Drain the potatoes and eggs, putting the potatoes into the bowl with the dressing and the eggs into a bowl of cold water.

10. Toss the potatoes in the warm dressing, then add to the salad bowl and toss everything together.

11. Peel and halve the eggs, then place them on the salad with the green beans and the salmon. Scatter over the olives and basil leaves before serving.

SERVES 2

GF

DF

Pan-fried sea bass with Mediterranean vegetables and crispy aubergine

It isn't the fish that takes time to cook here, it's the aubergines (eggplants), so get them cooking right at the start. Choosing baby aubergines and cutting them finely will speed up the process, but don't rush it – the oil needs to be really hot before you add the slices to the pan, or the aubergine flesh will just soak up the oil and be soft and greasy rather than crisp.

Olive oil, for frying
2 baby aubergines (eggplants)
  or 1 small aubergine
Zest and juice of 1 lemon
2 shallots
2 garlic cloves
1–2 red chillies
8–10 sundried tomatoes
125ml (½ cup) dry white wine
90ml (about ⅓ cup)
  vegetable stock
4 tbsp chopped canned
  tomatoes or passata
10 cherry tomatoes
2 tbsp pitted Kalamata olives
1 tbsp oregano leaves
4 small sea bass fillets,
  with skin
Sea salt and freshly ground
  black pepper
460g (2 cups) cooked Israeli
  or regular couscous, to serve
  (optional; find alternative
  if cooking gluten-free)

IF YOU HAVE MORE TIME...

...make the Mediterranean vegetables in advance. Any tomato-based sauce improves over time as the flavours develop, so it will be even more delicious.

1. Place a large frying pan (skillet) over a medium–high heat and coat the bottom of the pan with a tablespoon of olive oil.

2. While the oil is heating, finely slice the aubergines, then add them to the pan. Allow to cook for 2–3 minutes, tossing occasionally, until brown and crisp. Season with salt, pepper and half the lemon zest. Toss to combine, then drain the aubergines on kitchen paper (paper towel).

3. Meanwhile, peel and slice the shallots and slice or grate the garlic.

4. Wipe out the pan, return it to the heat and add a drizzle of olive oil. When hot, add the shallots and garlic and toss to coat.

5. Deseed and slice the chilli(es) and add to the pan along with the sundried tomatoes. Toss to combine, then reduce the heat to medium.

6. Add the wine and allow to bubble for 30 seconds, then add the vegetable stock and canned tomatoes and stir to combine. Remove the pan from the heat, then halve the cherry tomatoes and add them to the pan with the olives and oregano. Finish with a drizzle of olive oil and the remaining lemon zest.

7. Place a non-stick frying pan over a high heat and add a tablespoon of olive oil. While the oil is heating, gently score the skin on the sea bass fillets with a sharp knife. Season them and add to the pan, skin-side down. Cook for 1–2 minutes, until the skin is crisp, then flip. Drizzle the fish with olive oil, then squeeze over some lemon juice and remove the pan from the heat.

8. Warm up the couscous (if serving) and season generously with lemon juice.

9. Divide the couscous between two plates and surround it with the tomato sauce. Place the fish on top of the couscous, skin-side up, and place the crispy aubergine slices around the plate. Drizzle with olive oil before serving.

Steamed sea bream with ginger, soy, chilli and sesame fried shallots

Steaming is a quick and gentle way to cook fish, as well as being healthier than pan-frying. This method would work for any white fish, but you will need to adjust the time depending on the thickness of the fillets. You don't have to include the sesame fried shallots, but they do add a great crunch and nuttiness to the dish that makes it extra delicious.

1cm (½ inch) piece of fresh ginger
½ red chilli
4 x 120g (4½oz) sea bream or sea bass fillets
2 tbsp soy sauce
125ml (½ cup) fish stock, or water infused with 2 lime leaves
1 banana shallot (echalion) or 2 regular shallots
4 tbsp sesame oil
120g (1⅓ cups) Asian greens, e.g. choi sum or pak choi (choy sum or bok choy)

To serve
200g (1¼ cups) cooked rice
2 tbsp coriander (cilantro) leaves
Lime wedges

1. Start by lining a steamer with greaseproof paper, making sure that the paper comes up the sides so liquid cannot escape.

2. Fill the kettle with water and bring to the boil, then pour it into a saucepan and return to the boil over a medium heat.

3. Peel and grate the ginger and deseed and finely slice the chilli.

4. Put the fish fillets in the steamer, then add the ginger and chilli and pour over the soy sauce and fish stock (or infused water). Cover with the lid and place over the boiling water to steam for 4 minutes.

5. Meanwhile, peel and finely slice the shallot, add to a small saucepan with the sesame oil and place over a high heat. Allow to cook for 1 minute, or until the shallots begin to sizzle and turn golden brown.

6. Trim the Asian greens and add them to the steamer when the 4 minutes is up. Steam for a further 2 minutes.

7. Reheat the rice and divide between two shallow bowls.

8. Remove the fish from the steamer and place on top of the rice with the Asian greens. Drizzle over any liquid left in the steamer, then pour over the hot sesame oil and crispy shallots and sprinkle with the coriander leaves. Serve with lime wedges on the side.

TIP FOR SPEED
Use a teaspoon to peel the piece of ginger – it takes less time than using a knife and there is less waste.

Grilled sole with lentils, mushrooms and sorrel crème fraîche

You can make this flavour-packed dish with any mushrooms, but a mixture of different varieties and a handful of wild mushrooms, if you have them, will take it to the next level without any extra effort. The sorrel adds a lovely tang to the crème fraîche (sour cream), but if you can't get hold of it, use tarragon, dill, chervil or whichever soft herb you like.

160g (about 1½ cups) mixed mushrooms
100g (4oz) radishes, any leaves reserved
2 tbsp olive oil, plus extra for drizzling
4 x 160g (5½oz) lemon sole fillets
2 sprigs of thyme
50g (scant ½ stick) butter
120ml (½ cup) crème fraîche (sour cream)
2 tbsp sorrel or tarragon
Zest of ½ lemon and juice of whole lemon
1 x 250g (9oz) packet of cooked Puy lentils
2 tbsp cider or sherry vinegar
Sea salt and freshly ground black pepper

1. Preheat the grill (broiler) to high.

2. Slice or halve the mushrooms, then trim and halve the radishes, reserving the leaves (if any).

3. Drizzle a little oil over a roasting pan and lay the fish on it, skin side-down. Drizzle with olive oil, season with salt and pepper, then place under the hot grill for 4–5 minutes.

4. Meanwhile, place a large, non-stick frying pan (skillet) over a medium heat and add the 2 tablespoons olive oil. Once hot, add the radishes and fry for 1 minute, then add the mushrooms and thyme. Cook for 1–2 minutes, add the butter and continue to cook for a further 1–2 minutes.

5. Put the crème fraîche into a bowl and stir through the sorrel, the lemon zest and half the juice.

6. Heat the lentils as per the packet instructions, then season with salt and pepper and stir in the vinegar.

7. Spread the lentils over a serving plate and lay the sole fillets on top. Squeeze over the remaining lemon juice, add a dollop of sorrel crème fraîche to each fillet, then scatter over the radishes and mushrooms, and season with pepper. Sprinkle with the radish leaves (if any) before serving.

Chipotle-spiced trout with green apple and jalapeño salad

Chipotle peppers are, in fact, jalapeño chillies that have been left to ripen on the bush and then smoke-dried; they add a manageable heat and lovely smokiness to these trout fillets. The pickled jalapeños and tangy apples in the salad offset the fish beautifully. Get your fishmonger to butterfly the fish, or buy fillets instead, so that the preparation is kept to a minimum.

1 heaped tbsp chipotle paste
2 tbsp olive oil, plus extra
  for drizzling
4 butterflied trout or 8 fillets,
  with skin
1 tsp fennel seeds
1 tsp crushed pink
  peppercorns or freshly
  ground black pepper
2 tbsp chopped chives
2 tbsp chopped tarragon
6 tbsp natural (plain) yoghurt
2 tbsp chopped jalapeño
  chillies from a jar, plus
  1 tbsp of the juice
2 limes, halved
2 green apples
2 butter (Bibb) lettuces
Sea salt and freshly ground
  black pepper

1. Preheat the grill (broiler) to high.

2. Put the chipotle paste and measured olive oil into a bowl and mix well. Spread the paste over the fish skin, then sprinkle with the fennel seeds and crushed pink pepper.

3. Mix the herbs together and put half of them into a bowl with the yoghurt and jalapeño juice. Season with salt and pepper and stir well.

4. Drizzle a little oil over a roasting pan and lay the fish on it, skin side-up. Add the lime halves, cut-side up, and place under the hot grill for 6–7 minutes.

5. Meanwhile, finely slice the apples using a mandoline or blade side of a box grater and roughly tear the lettuce leaves.

6. Put the apple into a salad bowl with the lettuce, chopped jalapeños and the remaining herbs. Pour over the yoghurt dressing and toss well.

7. Place the trout fillets on four plates with a mound of salad and half a lime.

Cajun-spiced monkfish with chorizo and polenta

This is my take on 'shrimp and grits', a classic comfort food from the southern states of America, using monkfish instead of prawns, and chorizo instead of the more traditional bacon. I love modern-day Cajun cooking, which is full of gutsy, smoky flavours and plenty of heat, and I think these work especially well with the robust fish and creamy polenta.

1 tsp smoked paprika
1 tsp freshly ground
  black pepper
1 tsp dried oregano
2 x 180g (6¼oz) monkfish fillets
Olive oil, for frying
120g (4½oz) chorizo sausage,
  sliced into 5mm (¼ inch) rings
2–3 sprigs of thyme
1 lemon
1 heaped tbsp chipotle paste
1 heaped tbsp butter

For the polenta
90g (¾ stick) butter
90g (generous ½ cup) polenta
400ml (generous 1½ cups)
  vegetable stock or water
60g (2¼oz) Parmesan cheese
Sea salt and freshly ground
  black pepper

1. Start by making the polenta: put half the butter into a large saucepan and place it over a medium heat. When the butter has turned nut brown, add the polenta and stir to coat. Slowly pour in the stock while stirring with a whisk. The polenta will start to thicken as it heats.

2. Swap the whisk for a wooden spoon and keep stirring as the polenta cooks for 3 minutes. Add the remaining butter and grate in the Parmesan. Season with salt and pepper and stir thoroughly until the butter and cheese have melted. Cover with a lid to keep warm.

3. Put the smoked paprika, black pepper and oregano into a small bowl, mix well and use to coat the fish, pressing it into the flesh.

4. Place a large, non-stick frying pan (skillet) over a medium–high heat and coat the bottom of the pan with a drizzle of olive oil.

5. Once the oil is hot, add the fish and allow to cook for 3 minutes. Flip the fish and add the chorizo with the thyme sprigs. Continue to cook for 2 minutes, then squeeze over the lemon juice.

6. Divide the polenta between two plates. Remove the fish and chorizo from the pan and place on top of the polenta.

7. Turn the heat up under the frying pan and add the chipotle paste and butter. Once melted, drizzle over the fish and polenta before serving.

Fish and chips

It sounds impossible, but I really did pull off this recipe while locked down in Cornwall with my family. Okay, I was 39 seconds over the 10 minutes, but I blame my heckling daughters. The trick with the chips (french fries) is to make them as skinny as you can; this will help them cook through and crisp quickly. If you want to add traditional accompaniments, serve with gherkins (pickles) and mashed peas.

120g (1 cup) self-raising flour, plus extra for dredging
1 tsp baking powder
1 tsp curry powder
160ml (scant ⅔ cup) lager (beer)
1 egg white
Vegetable oil, for frying
2 x 170g (5¾oz) white fish fillets, e.g. cod or haddock
2 large Maris Piper or Russet potatoes
Sea salt

For the tartare sauce
2 heaped tbsp crème fraîche (sour cream)
2 heaped tbsp mayonnaise
8 mini gherkins (pickles)
Dash of Tabasco sauce
1 banana shallot (echalion) or 2 regular shallots
Zest and juice of ½ lemon, remaining ½ cut into wedges
Small handful of chopped parsley or dill (optional)

TIP FOR SPEED
You don't need to peel the potatoes – the skins are full of vitamins and will get really crisp and delicious when fried.

1. Preheat the oven to 140°C/120°C fan/275°F/Gas 1.

2. Sift the flour into a bowl and add the baking powder and ½ teaspoon of the curry powder. Pour in the lager and whisk vigorously to incorporate.

3. Put the egg white into a second bowl and whisk to soft peaks. Season with a pinch of salt, then pour into the flour mixture and whisk to combine.

4. Place a deep-sided frying pan (skillet) over a medium–high heat and coat the bottom generously with oil.

5. Put roughly 2 heaped tablespoons flour onto a plate and mix with the remaining ½ teaspoon curry powder.

6. Season the fish with salt, then dredge the fillets in the spiced flour, shaking off any excess. Lower the fillets into the beer batter and coat thoroughly.

7. Carefully place the fillets in the oil and cook for 1–2 minutes, basting the top of the fish. If the oil gets too hot, add a splash of cold oil and remove from the heat for a minute.

8. Meanwhile, peel the potatoes if you wish (see tip) and slice them into long skinny fries. Dry well on kitchen paper (paper towel).

9. Flip the fish and cook for a further 1–2 minutes, then remove from the oil and drain on kitchen paper. Place in the oven until ready to serve.

10. Add the fries to the hot oil and cook for 3–4 minutes, until golden and crisp.

11. Meanwhile, make the tartare sauce: combine the crème fraîche and mayonnaise in a small bowl. Roughly chop the gherkins and add to the bowl with a dash of Tabasco and a pinch of salt.

12. Peel and chop the shallot and add to the sauce with the lemon zest and juice.

13. Place the fish on two plates. Drain the fries on kitchen paper and stack them next to the fish. Serve with the tartare sauce and wedges of lemon.

Hot Goan fish curry

Cooking most curries takes a lot longer than ten minutes, but fish and shellfish cook so quickly that this one can be on the table in no time at all. Choose a firm white fish such as cod, haddock or halibut, throw in a mixture of shellfish, and let the distinct flavours of Goa – tamarind, coconut, curry leaves – do the rest of the work. Serve with rice, poppadoms and your favourite chutneys.

2 garlic cloves, peeled
3cm (1¼ inch) piece of
   fresh ginger, peeled
½ onion, peeled and quartered
4 tbsp vegetable oil
4–5 curry leaves
250g (9oz) skinless white fish,
   e.g. cod, haddock or halibut
500g (1lb 2oz) mussels
8 large raw prawns (shrimp)
½ tsp ground turmeric
1 tsp ground coriander
1 tsp ground cumin
3 cardamom pods
1 tsp chilli flakes
300ml (scant 1¼ cups)
   coconut milk
½ x 400g (15oz) can of
   cherry tomatoes
150ml (generous ½ cup)
   fish stock or water
140g (about 1 cup) unsalted
   cashew nuts
1 tsp tamarind paste
Sea salt and freshly ground
   black pepper

To serve
Cooked rice
Small handful of coriander
   (cilantro) leaves

1. Put the garlic, ginger and onion into a blender and blitz to a paste.

2. Place a large, non-stick frying pan (skillet) over a medium heat and add the oil. When hot, add the garlic paste along with the curry leaves and fry for 2 minutes.

3. Cut the fish into 3–4cm (1¼–1½ inch) pieces and wash any shellfish you are using.

4. Add the turmeric, coriander, cumin, cardamom pods and chilli flakes to the pan and season with salt and pepper. Stir and allow to cook for 1 minute before adding the fish.

5. After 2 minutes, add the shellfish, then pour in the coconut milk, cherry tomatoes and stock or water and bring to the boil.

6. Roughly chop the cashew nuts or crush them using a pestle and mortar. Add them to the pan and simmer for 5 minutes, then mix in the tamarind paste.

7. To serve, divide the rice between four bowls, then spoon over some curry and scatter with the coriander leaves.

Butterflied mackerel with crispy potatoes, leeks and romesco sauce

Romesco is one of my favourite no-cook sauces for maximum flavour with minimum effort. Here I've paired it with mackerel, but whole sardines, squid or prawns would also be delicious, as would pork or chicken, for that matter. Make a double quantity of the sauce and keep it in the fridge for up to a week, where it will intensify in flavour and be on hand for a second effortless meal. It freezes really well too.

400g (14oz) new potatoes
or leftover cooked potatoes
4 butterflied mackerel
or 8 fillets
400g (14oz) baby leeks,
trimmed
4 tbsp olive oil
1 tsp smoked paprika
1 red chilli, deseeded
and grated (see tip)
2–3 sprigs of rosemary,
leaves picked
1 lemon, cut into wedges,
to serve

For the romesco sauce
Pinch of saffron threads
1 tbsp sherry vinegar
2 garlic cloves
2½ tbsp olive oil
120g (4½oz) wood-roasted
(bell) peppers, from a jar
90g (scant 1 cup) toasted
flaked (sliced) almonds
Sea salt and freshly ground
black pepper

1. Preheat the grill (broiler) to high.

2. Fill the kettle with water and bring to the boil.

3. Cut the potatoes into rings 1cm (½ inch) thick and put them into a wide saucepan. Pour over just enough boiling water to cover, then cook for 3 minutes with the lid on.

4. Line the grill tray with foil or a silicone mat and put the mackerel on it, flesh-side down. Place under the hot grill for 8 minutes.

5. Add the leeks to the potatoes and cook for 2 minutes. Drain thoroughly and dry with kitchen paper (paper towel).

6. Meanwhile, make the romesco sauce: put the saffron into a small bowl with the vinegar and set aside. Peel the garlic, place in a small blender with the oil and blitz until just smooth. Add the peppers, almonds and saffron vinegar mix, season with salt and pepper and pulse until fully incorporated but still chunky.

7. Place a large frying pan (skillet) over a high heat and add the olive oil. When hot, add the drained or leftover potatoes and leeks and sprinkle with the paprika, grated chilli and rosemary. Cook until the potatoes are crisp and golden brown.

8. Divide the potatoes and leeks between four plates and place the grilled mackerel on top. Serve with the romesco sauce and lemon wedges on the side.

IF YOU HAVE MORE TIME…
…cook the fish and leeks on a barbecue for a more intense charred, smoky flavour.

TIP FOR SPEED
Instead of chopping the chilli, use a microplane to finely grate it. Remember to wash your hands thoroughly afterwards!

Smoked mackerel pâté with potato latkes

This pâté takes literally a matter of minutes to whip up, but I urge you to find the extra time to make the latkes that go with it. Latkes are shallow-fried potato cakes traditionally served at Hannukah, and they are every bit as delicious as they sound. They will take you over the ten-minute mark, though, so if you are pressed for time, sourdough toast would work very well too.

100g (scant ½ cup)
 cream cheese
2 tbsp creamed horseradish
2 smoked mackerel fillets,
 skinned
1 lemon

For the latkes (optional)
2 Maris Piper or Russet
 potatoes
1 banana shallot (echalion) or
 2 regular shallots
1 egg
1 heaped tbsp plain
 (all-purpose) flour
Pinch each of ground caraway
 seeds and white pepper
Vegetable oil, for frying
Sea salt and freshly ground
 black pepper

For the pickle salad
4 gherkins (pickles), plus a
 spoonful of the pickling liquid
⅓ cucumber
½ banana shallot (echalion)
 or 1 regular shallot
1 tbsp roughly chopped dill

To serve
2.5cm (1 inch) piece of fresh
 horseradish (optional)
1 lemon, cut into wedges

1. Put the cream cheese and creamed horseradish into a small bowl and mix well.

2. Using a fork, flake the mackerel flesh into thumbnail-sized pieces. Zest and juice the lemon over the fish before adding to the cream cheese mixture, then stir together thoroughly.

3. To make the latkes, use a box grater to coarsely grate the potatoes, then squeeze out any liquid by hand and put the grated potato into a bowl.

4. Peel and grate the shallot and add it to the potatoes along with the egg and flour. Season with a pinch of caraway and white pepper and mix everything well.

5. Place a large, non-stick frying pan (skillet) over a high heat and pour in a 2cm (¾ inch) depth of oil.

6. When the oil is hot (see tip), add heaped tablespoons of the latke mixture to the pan and flatten with the back of the spoon. Allow to fry for 2 minutes, until golden brown and crisp, then flip and cook for a further 2 minutes. Remove from the pan and drain on kitchen paper (paper towel), then season with salt and black pepper.

7. To make the pickle salad, slice the gherkins lengthways into 4–5 pieces and slice the cucumber into pieces roughly the same shape. Mix them together in a bowl. Peel the shallot, slice into rings and add to the bowl along with the chopped dill and spoonful of pickling liquid. Stir to combine.

8. Grate fresh horseradish (if using) over the pâté and serve with the latkes, the pickle salad and lemon wedges.

CHEF'S TIP

A clever way to work out when the oil is hot enough is to drop a popcorn kernel into the pan – when it pops, you are ready to fry. If you don't have any popcorn, use a cube of bread; you know the right temperature has been reached when the bread turns golden brown in 30 seconds.

Tuna katsu sandwich with ginger and apple slaw

I know this isn't a traditional katsu, but when it tastes this good, are you really going to complain? While you're at it, make double of the tonkatsu sauce. It's the Japanese equivalent of brown or steak sauce – sweet and tangy – and it goes brilliantly with burgers, pulled pork and bacon sandwiches, as well as the Japanese classic, pork tonkatsu. It will keep for at least a week if stored in the fridge in a sealed container.

Vegetable oil, for frying
2 heaped tbsp plain (all-purpose) flour
1 egg
60g (¾ cup) panko breadcrumbs
Dash of milk
2 x 170g (5¾oz) thick tuna steaks
180g (6¼oz) white cabbage
60g (2¼oz) pickled ginger, plus a splash of the pickling liquid
4 thick slices of white bloomer loaf, crusts removed
Freshly ground black pepper

For the tonkatsu sauce
125ml (½ cup) tomato ketchup
2 tbsp soy sauce
2 tbsp Worcestershire sauce
2 tbsp mirin
1 garlic clove, peeled
Pinch of chilli flakes

To serve
½ green apple (optional)
1 tsp toasted white sesame seeds or untoasted black sesame seeds (optional)
1 lime, cut into wedges

1. Place a heavy-based frying pan (skillet) over a high heat and coat the bottom of the pan with a thin layer of oil.

2. Put the flour, egg and panko breadcrumbs into three separate bowls. Season the flour with black pepper. Add a little milk to the egg and beat with a fork.

3. Dip each tuna steak in the flour, making sure it is well coated. Shake off any excess, then dip it in the egg followed by the breadcrumbs.

4. Place the steaks in the hot oil and cook for 1 minute on each side.

5. Meanwhile, finely slice the cabbage with a mandoline or the blade side of a box grater and combine in a bowl with the pickled ginger and pickling juice.

6. Make the tonkatsu sauce by combining the ketchup, soy sauce, Worcestershire sauce and mirin in a bowl. Grate in the garlic, add the chilli flakes and stir well.

7. To assemble each sandwich, spread the tonkatsu sauce on two slices of bread and top one of them with the cabbage slaw. Place the tuna steak on the slaw and sit the other slice of bread on top.

8. Finely slice the apple (if using) using a mandoline or sharp knife, then sprinkle with sesame seeds (if using).

9. Cut each sandwich in half and serve with the apple salad, lime wedges and any leftover tonkatsu sauce on the side.

Tuna panzanella

Every Tuscan grandmother will have a recipe for this great tomato and stale bread salad, but here is my super-quick version that you can make any time, whether you have day-old bread or not. No need to char and peel the peppers either – you can buy jars of incredible wood-roasted peppers preserved in olive oil, which can be sliced and added without any bother at all.

4 thick slices of sourdough bread
2 garlic cloves, peeled
2 tbsp red wine vinegar
400g (14oz) heritage (heirloom) tomatoes, at room temperature
240g (9oz) wood-roasted (bell) peppers, from a jar
½ red onion
Small handful of basil leaves
Vegetable oil, for frying
4 x 220g (7¾oz) tuna steaks
Sea salt and freshly ground black pepper

For the caper and anchovy dressing
½ red chilli
Zest and juice of 1 lemon
2 heaped tbsp capers
2 anchovy fillets in oil, chopped
3 tbsp olive oil

To serve
Olive oil, for drizzling
1 lemon, quartered

1. Place a griddle (grill) pan over a high heat.

2. Toast the bread in the toaster, then rub each slice with one of the garlic cloves.

3. Crush (mince) or grate the remaining garlic into a large bowl and add the vinegar.

4. Slice or chop the tomatoes, depending on their shape, and add them to the bowl. Cut the peppers into large pieces and add to the tomatoes. Peel and slice the onion and add to the bowl.

5. Tear the toasted bread into chunks and add to the salad along with half the basil leaves. Gently toss to combine.

6. To make the dressing, use a microplane to grate the chilli into a small bowl, then add the lemon zest and juice, the capers, chopped anchovies and olive oil. Mix well.

7. Brush the griddle pan with a little vegetable oil. Season the tuna steaks all over with salt and pepper, then griddle for 30 seconds on each side.

8. Arrange the panzanella salad on a serving plate and scatter over the remaining basil leaves.

9. Slice the tuna and place it on top of the salad. Dress with the caper and anchovy dressing and drizzle with a little olive oil. Serve with lemon wedges on the side.

Shrimp scampi with angel hair pasta

This is not what we Brits know as scampi – the breaded langoustine tails, beloved of pub menus, always served with chips (french fries) – but the Italian-American, buttery, garlicky prawn (shrimp) dish often served with very fine pasta, such as capellini or capelli d'angelo, otherwise known as angel hair. If you can't get hold of these, any quick-cooking long pasta will work, so try vermicelli, tagliolini or spaghettini instead.

1 tbsp olive oil, plus extra
   for frying and drizzling
2 banana shallots
2 garlic cloves, peeled
Pinch of chilli flakes
150g (1 cup) cherry tomatoes
60ml (¼ cup) white wine
60ml (¼ cup) vegetable
   or fish stock
Large handful of basil leaves
2 tbsp small capers
225g (8oz) very fine pasta,
   e.g. capellini, vermicelli
   or tagliolini
165g (5½oz) raw peeled prawns
   (shrimp)
Zest of 1 lemon, plus extra
   for serving
Sea salt and freshly ground
   black pepper

To serve
Freshly grated Parmesan
   cheese
Juice of 1 lemon

TIP FOR SPEED
To chop basil quickly, gather
the small leaves and roll
them up in the biggest leaf,
like a cigar, then chop with
a large knife.

1. Fill the kettle with water and bring to the boil, then half-fill a saucepan with it, season with salt and return to the boil.

2. Place a large, non-stick frying pan (skillet) over a medium heat and add 1 tablespoon olive oil.

3. While the oil is heating, peel and slice the shallots, then add them to the pan. Season with salt and pepper, then crush (mince) or grate the garlic into the pan. Sprinkle with the chilli flakes and cook for 2 minutes.

4. Meanwhile, halve the tomatoes and add them to the pan. Cook for 30 seconds, then deglaze the pan with the wine. Allow to bubble for 30 seconds, then add the stock and continue to reduce for 1–2 minutes.

5. Meanwhile, chop the basil leaves (see tip) and add to the sauce. Stir in the capers and remove the pan from the heat.

6. Add the pasta to the boiling water and cook as per the packet instructions, until al dente.

7. Place a second non-stick frying pan over a high heat and add a drizzle of olive oil.

8. While the oil is heating, season the prawns with salt and pepper. Add them to the pan and cook for approximately 30 seconds, until turning golden brown. Remove from the heat and turn the prawns over to cook in the residual heat.

9. Drizzle the prawns with olive oil and grate over the lemon zest, then add them to the sauce. Return the pan to the heat to warm through.

10. Drain the pasta and return to the pan. Add a drizzle of olive oil and toss to combine, then add the pasta to the pan of sauce and mix well.

11. To serve, divide the pasta between two plates and grate over some Parmesan. Add a little lemon zest and a squeeze of lemon juice before serving.

Clams and cannellini beans with parsley and shallot salad

Clams are packed full of flavour, which is what you need when time is short. They punch well above their weight and, with the garlic, sherry and parsley, really lift the more neutral beans. Another flavour heavyweight is black olive tapenade – keep a jar in the fridge and spread it on toast, as here, or stir through pasta sauces, salad dressings and marinades for a salty, earthy hit.

3 tbsp olive oil, plus extra
  for drizzling
3 garlic cloves
1kg (2lb 4oz) clams, washed
  and any with open or broken
  shells discarded
120ml (scant ½ cup) dry sherry
1 bunch of flat-leaf parsley
1 x 400g (15oz) can of
  cannellini or white (pinto)
  beans, drained and rinsed
1 tsp chilli flakes
1 banana shallot (echalion)
  or 2 regular shallots
1 heaped tbsp capers, plus a
  splash of the pickling liquid
2 small baguettes (French
  sticks) or 1 large focaccia
2 tbsp black olive tapenade

1. Preheat the grill (broiler) to high.

2. Place a large saucepan over a medium heat and add 3 tablespoons olive oil. While it is heating, peel and finely slice the garlic, then add to the pan and cook for 1 minute, until beginning to turn golden brown.

3. Add the clams and sherry. Cover with the lid and steam for 2–3 minutes, until the shells start to open. Discard any that remain closed.

4. Pick the parsley leaves and roughly chop the stalks.

5. Add the cannellini beans, chilli flakes and parsley stalks to the pan and bring to a simmer.

6. Add half the parsley leaves and mix well. Turn off the heat and cover with a lid to keep warm.

7. Peel and slice the shallot into rings, place in a bowl and toss with the remaining parsley leaves, the capers and their liquid and a drizzle of olive oil.

8. Cut the baguettes in half lengthways and toast under the hot grill, then spread with the tapenade.

9. Spoon the clams and beans into bowls before serving with the tapenade toast and parsley and shallot salad.

Herby mussels with Bloody Mary toasts

Mussels cook in less than five minutes, which makes them a brilliant choice for a ten-minute meal. I've added Bloody Mary toasts on the side, but to save time you can serve them with any crusty bread for mopping up the juices, then all you have to concentrate on is cooking the mussels. Double up the recipe if you are feeding more than two people and, obviously, leave the vodka out if you are making the toasts for kids.

Large handful of mixed soft herbs, e.g. parsley, tarragon and/or chives
1kg (2lb 4oz) cleaned mussels
100ml (scant ½ cup) white wine
1 celery stick
45g (1¾oz) fresh fennel
Olive oil, for dressing
Zest and juice of 1 lemon
2 thick slices of bread, e.g. sourdough, baguette (French stick) or white bloomer
100ml (scant ½ cup) double (heavy) cream
Pinch of chilli flakes
Sea salt and freshly ground black pepper

For the Bloody Mary paste
120g (4½oz) drained sundried tomatoes
1 tbsp grated horseradish, or 1 tbsp creamed horseradish, from a jar
4 tbsp hot sauce
1 tbsp Worcestershire sauce
2 tbsp vodka

1. Place a large saucepan over a medium heat to warm up.

2. Meanwhile, make the Bloody Mary paste: put the sundried tomatoes into a small blender, then add the horseradish, hot sauce, Worcestershire sauce and vodka and blitz to a coarse paste. Transfer to a small bowl and set aside.

3. Put the herbs into the empty blender (no need to rinse) with 2–3 tablespoons water and blitz until smooth.

4. Put the mussels into the hot pan with the wine, cover with a lid and cook for 4 minutes.

5. Meanwhile, finely slice the celery and fennel using a mandoline or speed peeler. Place in a bowl and dress with a dash of olive oil and the lemon zest and juice.

6. Toast the bread.

7. Stir the blitzed herbs and the cream into the mussels. Allow to cook for 30 seconds, until all the mussels are open (discard any that remain closed), then remove from the heat.

8. Spread the Bloody Mary paste on the toasts and top with the dressed fennel and celery and a pinch of chilli flakes.

9. Spoon the mussels into two bowls and serve with the Bloody Mary toasts on the side.

Crab and harissa tacos

Buying ready-picked white crab meat is such a good cheat here, and makes it easy to put these tacos together in minutes. The only cooking you need to do is warming up the tacos! I love the combination of sweet crab with hot, aromatic harissa, but you can use any chilli paste or hot sauce you like to get a kick, or leave it out altogether if you don't like the heat; the tacos will still be delicious.

200g (7oz) white crab meat
4 tbsp crème fraîche
  (sour cream)
1 Little Gem lettuce
Zest and juice of 1 lime
Small handful of coriander
  (cilantro) leaves
2 spring onions (scallions)
4 radishes
4 x 20cm (8 inch) soft corn
  tacos
2½ tbsp harissa paste
Sea salt and freshly ground
  black pepper
Lime wedges, to serve

1. Put the crab meat into a bowl and add the crème fraiche. Season with salt and pepper.

2. Shred the lettuce leaves and place in a salad bowl. Dress with the lime zest and juice, then sprinkle over half the coriander leaves. Slice the spring onions on the diagonal and add to the salad. Toss well.

3. Finely slice the radishes using a mandoline or very sharp knife.

4. Place a non-stick frying pan (skillet) over a medium heat and, when hot, warm the tacos for a few seconds, one at a time.

5. Spread some harissa paste in the centre of each taco, then place a spoonful of the salad on top, followed by a spoonful of the crab mixture. Top with the sliced radishes and remaining coriander, then fold and serve with lime wedges on the side.

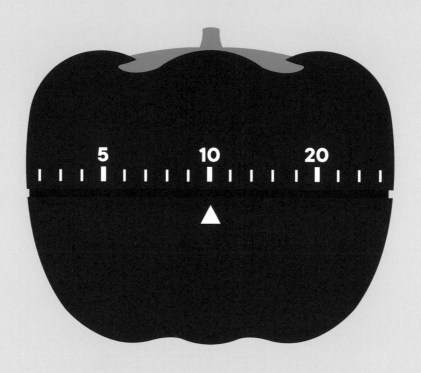

VEGETARIAN & VEGAN

SERVES 2

V

Tana's smoked red pepper soup with ricotta and tomato bruschette

I've borrowed one of Tana's family recipes here and adapted it so that it's ready in ten. The prep is quicker than the original, but the result is just as intense and satisfying. You can make it your own by stirring through extra ingredients after you've blitzed it – try cannellini beans, cooked chorizo or roast tomatoes for added texture and flavour. If you can't get hold of fresh oregano, you can use basil, thyme or mint.

1 litre (4 cups) vegetable stock
100ml (scant ½ cup) olive oil, plus extra for drizzling
1 red onion, peeled
4 garlic cloves, peeled
3 tbsp tomato purée (paste)
1 tsp sweet smoked paprika
200g (7oz) smoked piquillo peppers, from a jar
120g (4½oz) mixed heritage (heirloom) tomatoes
1 tbsp fresh oregano, thyme or basil leaves
2 slices of sourdough bread
3 tbsp ricotta cheese
Sea salt and freshly ground black pepper

CHEF'S TIP

Don't keep your fresh tomatoes in the fridge – they will have much more flavour if stored at room temperature.

1. Pour the vegetable stock into a saucepan, place over a high heat and bring to the boil.

2. Meanwhile, place a second saucepan over a high heat and add the olive oil.

3. Using a box grater, coarsely grate the red onion and finely grate the garlic. Put them both into the hot oil and cook for 3 minutes, stirring continuously.

4. Add the tomato purée and the smoked paprika to the pan and allow to cook for 1 minute.

5. Drain and roughly chop the piquillo peppers, then add them to the pan. Pour in the boiling stock and bring back to the boil for 4 minutes.

6. Slice or quarter the tomatoes according to size. Place in a bowl, then drizzle with olive oil, season with salt and pepper and sprinkle with the oregano leaves. Toss together.

7. Using a hand blender, blitz the soup until smooth, then season with salt and pepper.

8. Toast or grill the bread, then spread with the ricotta and spoon some of the tomatoes on top.

9. Serve the soup in warmed bowls with the bruschette on the side.

Warm tofu and green vegetable salad with ginger dressing

If you want to feel virtuous and healthy, this is the salad for you... Use any combination of green vegetables, and add seasonal leaves, such as wild garlic, sorrel or pea shoots, when available. If tofu isn't your thing, you could poach some chicken or steam some fish to serve with the veg instead. Furikake, a Japanese seasoning made from seaweed and sesame seeds, finishes the dish beautifully with a hit of savoury umami.

1 bunch of asparagus, trimmed
240g (8½oz) purple sprouting broccoli
2 heads of pak choi (bok choy)
100g (1¾ cups) sugarsnap peas or mangetout (snow peas)
100g (⅓ cup) edamame beans
300g (11oz) firm tofu
½ bunch of coriander (cilantro)
2 spring onions (scallions), halved and finely sliced lengthways
1 tbsp furikake seasoning or vegetarian equivalent

For the ginger dressing
120ml (½ cup) light soy sauce or tamari
4 tbsp rice wine vinegar
2 tbsp pickled ginger, finely chopped
Pinch of caster sugar

1. Fill the kettle with water and bring to the boil. Pour into a saucepan and return to the boil.

2. Trim the asparagus and broccoli, and remove the base of the pak choi. Put the asparagus and broccoli into the boiling water. Place the pak choi, sugarsnaps and edamame beans in a steamer, sit it over the water and cover with a lid.

3. Cut the tofu into large cubes and add them to the steaming vegetables for 2–3 minutes.

4. Meanwhile, put all the ginger dressing ingredients into a clean screwtop jar and shake until combined.

5. After 2–3 minutes, drain the asparagus and broccoli and put them into a salad bowl with the steamed veg and beans and the tofu. Add the ginger dressing and toss together.

6. Divide the warm salad between two bowls and scatter with the coriander leaves, spring onions and furikake seasoning before serving.

White bean skordalia with grilled aubergine, feta and dukkah

Skordalia is a thick Greek dip that is traditionally made with mashed potatoes or stale bread mixed with garlic and olive oil. Here I've replaced those carbs with cooked white beans straight from the can, which not only makes the recipe quicker, but also lighter and healthier. To make a meal of it, I grill some aubergines and crumble over some feta cheese, but you could just serve it as a dip with toasted pitta crisps or crusty bread.

1 large aubergine (eggplant)
2 garlic cloves, peeled
4 tbsp olive oil, plus extra
   for frying and drizzling
200g (7oz) canned chopped
   tomatoes
Pinch of chilli flakes
½ tsp ground cinnamon
1 red onion
1 x 400g (15oz) can of
   cannellini or white (pinto)
   beans, drained and rinsed
80g (3¼oz) feta cheese or
   vegetarian equivalent
1 tbsp dukkah
1 tbsp coriander (cilantro)
   leaves
1 tbsp mint leaves
Sea salt and freshly ground
   black pepper
2 warm flatbreads, to serve

1. Place a griddle (grill) pan over a high heat.

2. Discard the stem from the aubergine, then cut in half lengthways. Cut each half into 3 wedges. Place the wedges in the hot pan and cook for 3–4 minutes on each cut side.

3. Meanwhile, crush (mince) or grate one of the garlic cloves into a small pan containing a little olive oil and place it over a medium heat. After about 30 seconds, add the chopped tomatoes, chilli flakes and cinnamon and leave to simmer.

4. When the aubergine wedges are ready, put them into a bowl and cover so that they steam and cook a little further.

5. Peel and slice the red onion into rings 5mm (¼ inch) thick. Separate the rings, place them in the griddle pan and cook until slightly softened and lightly coloured. Add them to the bowl of aubergine.

6. Using a small blender, pulse the white beans and remaining garlic clove with the 4 tablespoons oil. Season with salt and pepper, then warm in a small pan over a low heat.

7. Remove the tomatoes from the heat and mix with the aubergine and onion.

8. Divide the skordalia between two plates, then pile the tomato-dressed aubergine alongside. Crumble the feta over the aubergine, then sprinkle the dukkah and herbs over the top. Drizzle with a little oil before serving with the warm flatbreads.

IF YOU HAVE MORE TIME...
...dry-roast the dukkah in a frying pan (skillet) for 1–2 minutes before using – it will enliven the spices and add more flavour to the finished dish.

California-style sweetcorn chowder

I spend a lot of time in LA and have come to love the laid-back California style of cooking and some of the ingredients that can be accessed there. For example, Hatch chillies, which come from New Mexico and have an earthy flavour and similar heat to jalapeños, and Mexican cheeses, such as cotija. If you aren't living in the United States, you might be able to get hold of these items online, but if not, I've suggested alternatives. Be warned that there is a lot of prep in this recipe, so it will probably take a bit longer than ten minutes.

½ large onion, peeled
110g (¾ cup) roasted red (bell) peppers from a jar, deseeded
175g (6oz) Maris Piper or Yukon Gold potatoes, scrubbed
5 tbsp unsalted butter
225g (8oz) Hatch green chillies, chopped, or 100g (4oz) jalapeño chillies, roughly chopped (deseed if you want a milder heat)
420g (3 cups) canned or frozen sweetcorn, drained or defrosted
2 tsp garlic paste
1 tbsp ground cumin
1 tsp dried chipotle chilli flakes or 2 tsp chipotle paste
875ml–1 litre (3½–4 cups) vegetable stock
250ml (1 cup) whole milk
250ml (1 cup) double (heavy) cream
100g (4oz) soft goats' cheese
Sea salt and freshly ground black pepper

To serve
Large handful of coriander (cilantro), chopped
Cotija or feta cheese, crumbled (optional)
Lime wedges
Crunchy bread

1. Start by roughly chopping the onion and red peppers and coarsely grating the potatoes.

2. Place a wide saucepan over a high heat and add the butter. When the butter is bubbling and starting to brown, add the prepared vegetables along with the chopped chillies, sweetcorn, garlic paste, ground cumin and chipotle flakes or paste, then season with salt and pepper and cook for 2–3 minutes.

3. Pour in the vegetable stock, milk and the cream, cover and bring to the boil. Reduce to a simmer and cook for 3–4 minutes, stirring occasionally.

4. Whisk in the goats' cheese until melted, adding more stock or cream if the soup seems too thick.

5. Check the seasoning, then ladle into warm bowls and serve with the coriander leaves and cotija or feta (if using) sprinkled on top. Offer the lime wedges separately, and serve with crunchy bread.

Rainbow salad with spiced granola and golden citrus vinaigrette

You don't really need me to tell you how to put together a ten-minute salad – there are so many different possibilities, and I trust you to combine the ingredients you like in the right proportions. Where I come in is to introduce you to new dressings and elements you might not have tried before, such as this turmeric and orange dressing and spiced oat, nut and seed mix, which will take your salad to the next level. The recipe can be made dairy-free if the cheese is left out.

250g (6 cups) mixed green salad leaves
80g (2 cups) spinach leaves
4 small red or candy-striped beetroot (beets), peeled and finely sliced
4 carrots, shaved into ribbons
8–10 cherry tomatoes, halved
70g (½ cup) crumbled feta, goats' cheese or vegetarian alternative (optional)
Sea salt

For the spiced granola
2 tbsp pumpkin seeds
2 tbsp sunflower seeds
2 tbsp chopped pistachios
4 tbsp rolled oats
Pinch of chilli flakes
Pinch of sea salt
2 tbsp maple syrup
2 egg whites

For the golden citrus vinaigrette
1 tsp freshly grated turmeric root or ½ tsp ground turmeric
1 tsp freshly grated ginger
2 tbsp honey
Juice and zest of 1 orange
¼ tsp freshly ground black pepper
4 tbsp olive oil

1. Start by making the spiced granola: put all the ingredients for it into a bowl and stir well. (Any leftover egg yolks can be used in one of the omelette recipes or the Chocolate and Honeycomb Mousse, page 247.)

2. Tip the mixture into a non-stick frying pan (skillet) and cook over a high heat for 3 minutes, stirring regularly, until lightly browned and crisp. Set aside and allow to cool.

3. Meanwhile, put all the vinaigrette ingredients, apart from the oil, into a blender and blitz until smooth. Then, with the blender running, slowly pour in the olive oil in a steady stream until emulsified, or incorporate it 1 tablespoon at a time.

4. Put the salad leaves into a large bowl, drizzle over 1–2 tablespoons of the dressing and season with salt.

5. Add the spinach, beetroot slices, carrots and tomatoes to the salad bowl, then add a handful of the granola and the crumbled feta (if using). Toss the salad well before serving.

Scrunched kale, pear and Brie salad with walnut dressing

When I say scrunched kale, I mean that the leaves are crushed with tongs while being blanched for a few seconds. This softens them enough to be eaten in a salad without any further cooking. A similar result can be achieved by massaging the leaves by hand, but scrunching my way is quicker and more effective. Make sure you dry the leaves thoroughly afterwards, though. You can leave out the Brie to make this recipe vegan, and swap the walnuts for pistachios or almonds, if you prefer.

200g (3 cups) chopped kale
2 tsp fennel seeds
250g (9oz) ready-cooked Puy or beluga lentils (optional)
2 tbsp red wine vinegar
4 tbsp olive oil
2 ripe pears
120g (4½oz) cooked beetroot (beets)
200g (7oz) Brie cheese, sliced, or vegetarian equivalent
2 tbsp maple syrup

For the walnut dressing
100g (1 cup) walnuts
½ garlic clove, peeled
1 tbsp red wine vinegar
3 tbsp olive oil
3 tbsp crème fraîche (sour cream)
Sea salt and freshly ground black pepper

1. Fill the kettle with water and bring to the boil.

2. Put the kale into a colander over a large bowl and pour in the boiling water until the leaves are covered. Use a pair of tongs to scrunch the leaves, keeping them moving for a few seconds, then hold the colander under running cold water for a few seconds to refresh them. Dry thoroughly on kitchen paper (paper towel).

3. To make the walnut dressing, put the walnuts into a blender and blitz until finely chopped. Add the garlic, vinegar and olive oil, season with salt and pepper, then add 3 tablespoons water and blitz until smooth. Blend in the crème fraîche and a little more water if required.

4. Put the fennel seeds into a small, dry frying pan (skillet) and place over a medium heat for 1–2 minutes, until toasted and aromatic.

5. Put the kale leaves into a salad bowl with the lentils (if using) and dress with the vinegar, olive oil and toasted fennel seeds, scrunching the kale with the tongs until thoroughly coated.

6. Smear the walnut dressing over four plates, then pile the dressed kale on top.

7. Slice the pears into sixths and remove the cores, then slice the beetroot and Brie.

8. Arrange the pear, beetroot and Brie slices on top of the kale and drizzle with the maple syrup before serving.

Gado gado salad with peanut sauce

This chopped salad comes from Indonesia, where *gado gado* means 'mix mix', a good description of what ends up in the salad bowl – colourful raw vegetables, noodles, tofu, crackers and herbs with a sharp peanut dressing. If you have more time or handy leftovers, you can add cooked veg too, such as green beans, edamame or new potatoes. Vermicelli rice noodles take no time to cook, but you can buy them pre-cooked for even less bother.

2 eggs
100g (4oz) rice noodles
140g (4¾oz) firm tofu
90g (3½oz) cucumber
Vegetable oil, for frying
60g (generous ½ cup)
    beansprouts, ready to eat
60g (⅔ cup) shredded
    Chinese or napa cabbage
60g (scant ½ cup) halved
    cherry tomatoes
4 radishes, sliced
Small handful of prawn
    crackers
¼ bunch of coriander (cilantro)
¼ bunch of mint, leaves picked

For the peanut sauce
1 tbsp kecap manis
1 tbsp fish sauce
Thumb-sized piece of fresh
    ginger, peeled and finely
    grated
Zest and juice of 2 limes
150ml (generous ½ cup)
    coconut milk
4 tbsp peanut butter

1. Fill the kettle with water and bring to the boil.

2. Pour half the water into a small saucepan and bring back to the boil. Add the eggs and cook for 6 minutes.

3. Pour the remaining water over the rice noodles in a heatproof bowl. Cover and leave to soak for 3 minutes before draining.

4. Meanwhile, chop the tofu into large cubes and thickly slice the cucumber.

5. Now make the peanut dressing: put the kecap manis, fish sauce, ginger, lime zest and juice of 1 lime into a blender, add the coconut milk and blitz until smooth. Add the peanut butter and pulse until fully incorporated and smooth.

6. Place a small, non-stick frying pan (skillet) over a medium heat and add a little oil. When hot, add the tofu cubes and fry for 2 minutes, until golden brown.

7. When the eggs are cooked, hold them under running cold water until cool enough to handle, then peel off the shells. Once peeled, slice in half lengthways.

8. Smear the sauce around the bottom of a deep serving bowl and arrange all the ingredients in clock sections, starting at the top (12 o'clock) and working around the bowl. Squeeze the remaining lime juice over everything, then sprinkle with the coriander sprigs and mint leaves before serving.

Sesame-grilled tofu with miso mayonnaise

Tofu can, let's face it, be quite bland, but not if you coat it with sesame seeds, pan-fry it and serve it with this punchy miso and Marmite mayonnaise. A sprinkle of the Japanese pepper mix shichimi togarashi finishes it off beautifully. Serve with Asian greens that have been wilted in the pan used to cook the tofu and steamed rice. Use soya milk instead of egg white if you want to make the dish vegan.

280g (10oz) firm tofu
1 tbsp soy sauce
1 egg white
60g (scant ½ cup) sesame seeds
Vegetable oil, for frying
1 tsp pickled ginger
1 tbsp coriander (cilantro) leaves
Pinch of shichimi togarashi

For the miso mayonnaise
1 tsp white miso paste
½ tsp Marmite (nutritional yeast)
2 tbsp mayonnaise

1. Start by making the miso mayonnaise: put the miso paste and Marmite into a bowl and stir to combine, then add the mayonnaise and stir until smooth.

2. Cut the tofu into 7–8 thick slices and drizzle with the soy sauce.

3. Gently whisk the egg white until frothy.

4. Dip the tofu pieces in the egg white, then coat in the sesame seeds.

5. Place a non-stick frying pan (skillet) over a medium heat and add enough oil to coat the bottom of the pan. When hot, add the tofu pieces and fry for about 30 seconds on each side, until toasted and golden.

6. Meanwhile, roughly chop the pickled ginger and mix it with the coriander leaves.

7. Remove the tofu from the pan and drain on kitchen paper (paper towel), before placing on a serving plate with a spoonful of the miso mayonnaise on top of each piece. Garnish the tofu with the ginger and coriander mix and sprinkle the togarashi seasoning over the tofu and mayonnaise before serving.

Beetroot falafel wraps with green tahini

1 x 400g (15oz) can of chickpeas (garbanzos), drained and rinsed
1 garlic clove, peeled
1 tsp fennel seeds
1 tsp cumin seeds
1 tsp chilli flakes
1 tsp sea salt
1 tsp bicarbonate of soda (baking soda)
120g (4½oz) cooked beetroot (beets)
60g (generous ½ cup) gram (chickpea) flour
Vegetable oil, for frying
1 tsp toasted sesame seeds

For the green tahini
Small handful of mixed soft herbs (mint, coriander/cilantro and parsley)
1 garlic clove, peeled
Zest and juice of 1 lemon
4 tbsp tahini paste
100g (⅖ cup) natural (plain) yoghurt
Sea salt and freshly ground black pepper

To serve
¼ red onion, peeled and sliced
Juice of ½ lemon
Pinch of sumac
2 flatbreads or tortillas
1 tbsp mint leaves
1 tbsp coriander (cilantro) leaves
2 tbsp pomegranate seeds (optional)

These falafels definitely push the ten-minute limit, but they are so easy to make and delicious to eat, I had to include them. It's the number of ingredients that will slow you down, so make sure you have them all assembled, weighed out and prepped before you start cooking. Replace the natural yoghurt in the green tahini with plain soya or coconut yoghurt to make it vegan.

1. Start by making the green tahini dressing: put the herbs, garlic, lemon zest and juice into the blender and blitz until smooth. Add the tahini and yoghurt and season with salt and pepper. Add a little warm water if it is too thick, then decant the sauce into a bowl.

2. Using the same blender (no need to wash it), make the beetroot falafels: put the chickpeas into the blender with the garlic, fennel and cumin seeds, chilli flakes, salt and bicarbonate of soda and blend until coarsely chopped.

3. Grate in the beetroot and pulse to combine. Decant the mixture into a mixing bowl and fold in the chickpea flour.

4. Place a large, non-stick frying pan (skillet) over a medium heat and add just enough oil to coat the bottom of the pan.

5. When the oil is hot, add spoonfuls of the beetroot mixture and flatten gently with the back of the spoon. Cook for 2 minutes on each side, then drain on kitchen paper (paper towel). Put the hot falafels into a bowl with the sesame seeds, season with black pepper and toss to combine.

6. Put the sliced onion into a bowl, add the lemon juice and sumac and mix together.

7. Warm the flatbreads for a few seconds in a dry frying pan over a high heat, then transfer to plates and spread a generous layer of the green tahini on each one. Divide the falafels between the plates and scatter the onion, mint, coriander and pomegranate seeds (if using) over the top.

CHEF'S TIP
Put your falafels into the hot frying pan in a clockwise circle, starting at twelve o'clock. When 2 minutes is up, start turning them over in the same order they were added to ensure even cooking across the whole batch.

Root vegetable bhaji 'burgers' with green chilli yoghurt and mango chutney

Sick of lentil burgers? Try this – a crisp onion, carrot and parsnip bhaji served in a burger bun with hot and sweet sauces and a bunch of fresh coriander leaves. Trust me, it's incredible. There's no need to peel the carrot or parsnip for these, which not only saves prep time, but also ensures you get all the nutrition and fibre that the skin contains.

Vegetable oil, for frying
150g (1½ cups) gram (chickpea) flour
1 tsp ground turmeric
1 tsp ground cumin
2 tsp dried chilli flakes
1 parsnip
1 carrot
2 red onions, peeled
⅓ bunch of coriander (cilantro)
1 green chilli, deseeded if you want a milder heat
140g (generous ½ cup) natural (plain) yoghurt
4 burger buns
160g (5½oz) mango chutney
Sea salt and freshly ground black pepper

1. Pour a 6cm (2½ inch) depth of vegetable oil into a saucepan and place over a medium–high heat.

2. While the oil is heating, put the gram flour, turmeric, cumin and chilli flakes into a bowl and add 160ml (scant ⅔ cup) cold water. Use a whisk to mix thoroughly.

3. Using a box grater, grate the parsnip and carrot straight into the batter.

4. Chop the onions in half and slice finely. Break the slices up before adding them to the batter. Season with salt and pepper.

5. Pick the leaves off the coriander stalks and put half of them aside for later. Place the stalks and remaining leaves in a blender, add the green chilli and yoghurt, then blitz until smooth.

6. Divide the thick batter into four in the bowl, and, when the oil is hot enough (see tip on page 168), spoon each quarter into the pan and press down a little with the spoon until each bhaji is no more than 3–4cm (1¼–1½ inches) thick. Fry for 4–5 minutes, until golden brown, then drain the bhajis on kitchen paper (paper towel).

7. Meanwhile, slice the burger buns open, then spread the bottom halves with the chilli yoghurt and the lids with mango chutney. Place the bhajis on the yoghurt and garnish with the remaining coriander leaves before putting the lids on top.

TIP FOR SPEED
There's no need to waste time peeling the carrots and parsnips – just give them a good scrub before grating them.

V

VG

GF

DF

Bang bang cauliflower

Something happens to cauliflower when you stir-fry or roast it at high temperatures – it becomes nutty and sweet as it caramelises and seems like a different vegetable from its boiled or steamed cousins. I've borrowed the sauce here from bang bang chicken, a Chinese dish from Sichuan province, which has been much adulterated in the US. It should be sweet and hot, wherever it's from.

½ cauliflower, cut into florets (flowerets), tender leaves (if any) reserved
1 heaped tbsp rice flour
2 tbsp vegetable oil
½ small red onion
2–3cm (¾–1¼ inch) piece of fresh ginger
2 garlic cloves
2 tbsp sesame oil
Small handful coriander (cilantro) leaves

For the bang bang sauce
2 tbsp maple syrup or agave syrup
2 tbsp Cholula or sriracha hot sauce
4 tbsp sweet chilli sauce

1. Start by making the bang bang sauce: put all the ingredients for it into a bowl and stir until fully combined. Set aside until needed.

2. Toss the cauliflower florets in the rice flour.

3. Place a wok over a high heat and add the vegetable oil. When hot, add the cauliflower florets and stir-fry for 3 minutes. Add the reserved cauliflower leaves (if any) and stir-fry for another 3–4 minutes.

4. Meanwhile, peel and slice the onion; peel the ginger and cut into small strips; peel and crush (mince) the garlic.

5. Place a small saucepan over a medium heat and add the sesame oil. When hot, add the onion, garlic and ginger and cook, stirring occasionally for 2 minutes, until soft.

6. Remove the pan from the heat and stir in the bang bang sauce.

7. Pour the onion mixture into the wok and stir until the cauliflower is fully coated. Pour the cauliflower into a serving dish, sprinkle with the coriander leaves and serve with boiled rice and green vegetables.

Stilton and spinach-stuffed mushrooms with watercress, chicory and walnut salad

It turns out that life is not too short to stuff a mushroom... at least, not when it takes only ten minutes! Make sure the oven is really hot before you grill the mushrooms so that the cheese melts really quickly. You can double this recipe to serve four people, but the prep will take longer and therefore push you over the ten-minute mark.

4 large Portobello mushrooms
3 tbsp olive oil, plus extra
    for frying
1 garlic clove, peeled and
    crushed (minced)
100g (4oz) frozen leaf spinach,
    defrosted and excess water
    squeezed out
2 tbsp cream cheese
4 tbsp double (heavy) cream
40g (1½oz) Stilton or other
    hard blue cheese
4 tbsp fresh breadcrumbs
1 tbsp fresh oregano leaves
Sea salt and freshly ground
    black pepper

For the salad
Large handful of mixed
    salad leaves
2 tbsp walnuts
2 tbsp walnut oil
Juice of 1 lemon,
    plus a little zest

1. Preheat the grill (broiler) to high.

2. Remove and chop the mushroom stalks.

3. Place a non-stick frying pan (skillet) over a medium heat and add a little olive oil. When hot, cook the mushroom caps for 3 minutes, placing a clean, heavy-based saucepan on top of them to speed up the cooking process.

4. While the mushrooms are cooking, warm a tablespoon of the olive oil in a small saucepan over a medium heat. Add the crushed garlic and mushroom stalks and cook for 1 minute.

5. Roughly chop the defrosted spinach and add it to the pan with the garlic. Allow to cook for 1 minute, then add the cream cheese and cream. Season with salt and pepper, stirring until thoroughly combined. Reduce the heat to low.

6. Turn the mushrooms over and cook for a further minute.

7. Remove the mushrooms from the pan and put them, gill-side up, in a roasting pan. Fill each one with the spinach mixture, then crumble the blue cheese over the top.

8. Mix the remaining olive oil with the breadcrumbs and press them on top of the cheese. Scatter the oregano leaves over the top and grate over a little lemon zest. Place the roasting pan under the hot grill for 2 minutes, or until the crumbs turn golden brown.

9. Put the salad leaves into a bowl and crumble in the walnuts. Add the walnut oil and lemon juice and zest and toss gently to coat.

10. Transfer the mushrooms to plates and serve with the salad.

Porcini 'meatball' sub

Porcini powder is a secret weapon in vegetarian and vegan cooking because it's full of umami, that elusive fifth taste, which can be hard to come by when you cut out meat and cheese. Make it yourself by grinding dried porcini mushrooms to a powder, or buy it online, where you can also find vegan Worcestershire sauce. Swap the basil for thyme, marjoram or fresh oregano if you prefer.

1 egg
200g (7oz) soya mince
 (soy granules)
1 tsp porcini powder
1 tbsp vegan Worcestershire
 sauce
Pinch of chilli flakes
70g (generous ½ cup) fresh
 breadcrumbs
3 tbsp olive oil, plus extra
 for drizzling
2 garlic cloves
200g (7oz) mixed mushrooms
1 x 400g (15oz) can of
 chopped tomatoes
1 baguette (French stick)
Small handful of basil leaves
125g (generous 1 cup) grated
 mozzarella cheese
Sea salt and freshly ground
 black pepper

1. Preheat the grill (broiler) to high.

2. Crack the egg into a large bowl and add the soya mince, porcini powder, Worcestershire sauce and chilli flakes. Gently mix everything together, then fold in the breadcrumbs.

3. Place a large, non-stick frying pan (skillet) over a high heat and add the olive oil.

4. Using your hands, divide the breadcrumb mixture into 12 equal pieces, then roll into balls. Add them to the hot oil.

5. While the balls are frying, peel the garlic and grate straight into the pan. Mix with the 'meatballs' and allow to colour for 2 minutes, shaking the pan occasionally.

6. Meanwhile, roughly chop the mushrooms and add them to the pan. Allow to cook for 3 minutes.

7. Add the chopped tomatoes and allow to boil rapidly for 2 minutes. Remove from the heat and season with salt and pepper.

8. Slice the baguette in half lengthways along the top but not all the way through, then open it out like a book.

9. Spoon the 'meatballs' and sauce into the baguette and sprinkle over the basil leaves and mozzarella.

10. Place the baguette under the grill until the cheese has melted and the edges of the bread are lightly toasted.

11. Serve on a board with a bread knife alongside, or slice into four portions before serving with a green salad.

Cauliflower steaks with almonds and green sauce

Cauliflower steaks make an excellent plant-based main course, especially when served with a piquant salsa verde and butter-toasted almonds spooned over the top. You can double up the recipe. but be aware that the steaks will get smaller as you move away from the centre of the cauliflower. Serve them with roasted new potatoes and a bitter green salad to offset the buttery sauce.

1 cauliflower
40g (⅓ stick) butter
1 bay leaf
2 garlic cloves, peeled
  and crushed with the
  blade of a chef's knife
30g (⅓ cup) flaked (sliced)
  or chopped almonds
1 tsp cumin seeds
1 banana shallot (echalion) or
  2 regular shallots
3 tbsp flat-leaf parsley leaves

For the green sauce
2 tbsp mint leaves
2 tbsp dill
1 tbsp oregano leaves
  or ½ tsp dried oregano
2 tbsp red wine vinegar
2 tsp dark brown sugar
2 tsp Dijon mustard
80ml (scant ⅓ cup) olive oil
Sea salt and freshly ground
  black pepper

1. Start by cutting two thick steaks from the centre of the cauliflower (use the remaining florets/flowerets for the Bacon Cauliflower Cheese on Toast on page 40 or the Bang Bang Cauliflower on page 206).

2. Place the steaks in a shallow frying pan (skillet) that has a lid and add half the butter, the bay leaf, crushed garlic and 100ml (scant ½ cup) water. Cover and place over a high heat for 6–7 minutes, or until the steaks are just soft.

3. While the cauliflower is cooking, put the almonds into a saucepan with the remaining butter and cumin seeds and place over a medium heat. Cook for 2–3 minutes, stirring occasionally, until golden brown.

4. Peel the shallot and slice it into rings. Set aside for later.

5. Remove the lid from the cauliflower pan so that the liquid can reduce a little.

6. When the almonds are golden brown, set them aside in the pan. Turn the cauliflower steaks and allow the liquid to reduce a little more.

7. Meanwhile, put all the ingredients for the green sauce into a blender and blitz until smooth.

8. Mix the parsley leaves and shallot rings together and stir in 2 tablespoons of the green sauce.

9. When the cauliflower steaks are ready, place them on two plates and spoon the almonds in butter and any butter from the cauliflower pan over the top. Divide the parsley and shallot mixture between the two plates and drizzle with the remaining green sauce before serving.

Speedy lentil dhal with paneer and coconut sambal

Using pre-cooked lentils for this dhal considerably speeds up the recipe, but you still need to cook the lentils further to break them down, so get them on first before turning your attention to the temper. And by temper, I don't mean my angry outbursts when forced to eat inedible food, but the aromatic mixture of garlic, spices and curry leaves cooked in oil or ghee that is poured over many Indian dishes before serving. Eat this dhal with rice, poppadoms or the Indian Rice Flour Pancakes on page 31.

1 x 400ml (13½fl oz) can
   of coconut milk
1 tsp ground turmeric
750g (3¾ cups) cooked lentils
   (yellow, red or black)
120ml (½ cup) vegetable oil
2 tbsp chopped garlic
2 tbsp cumin seeds
1 red chilli, deseeded if you
   want a milder heat, diced
2 tbsp coriander seeds
2 tbsp curry leaves
100g (⅔ cup) cherry tomatoes
250g (9oz) paneer
150g (5oz) baby spinach leaves
4 tbsp coriander (cilantro)
   leaves

For the coconut sambal (optional)
1 lime
4 tbsp desiccated (shredded)
   coconut
1 tsp mustard seeds
4 tbsp natural (plain) yoghurt
Pinch of chilli flakes
Sea salt

1. Pour the coconut milk into a large saucepan over a medium heat. Rinse the can with 200ml (¾ cup) water, add to the pan and bring to a simmer. Add the turmeric and cooked lentils and allow to cook for 8 minutes over a low heat, stirring from time to time.

2. While the dhal is cooking, make the coconut sambal: zest and juice the lime and mix into the coconut. Stir through the mustard seeds and yoghurt, then season with salt and a pinch of chilli flakes. Set aside until needed.

3. Pour the vegetable oil into a small saucepan and place over a medium heat. When hot, add the chopped garlic. Once the garlic starts to brown a little, add the cumin seeds, diced red chilli, coriander seeds and curry leaves and allow to cook for 1 minute.

4. Halve the cherry tomatoes, add them to the oil, then turn the heat as low as it will go.

5. Cut the paneer into 2cm (¾ inch) cubes.

6. Place a frying pan (skillet) over a high heat and dry-fry the paneer until it is browned all over, then add it to the spice mixture.

7. Fold the baby spinach leaves through the lentils until just wilted.

8. Ladle the dhal into four warm bowls, spoon the paneer and temper over the top and garnish with the coriander leaves. Serve with the coconut sambal in a small dish on the side.

Sticky apricot tagine

Tagines are typically braised very slowly to allow intense flavours to develop, but given the ten-minute challenge, I've had to speed up the process and pack this vegetarian version with aromatics and spices from the get-go. Adding butter towards the end of the cooking time adds richness, but it can be left out if you are vegan and the finished dish won't suffer for it.

4 apricot halves (from
  a can or jar), drained,
  liquid reserved
75g (3oz) cherry tomatoes
  on the vine
4 tbsp pomegranate molasses
Olive oil, for frying
1 red onion, peeled and
  quartered
1 fennel bulb, sliced
  on a mandoline
3 carrots, thickly sliced
  at an angle
1 tbsp garlic purée
275g (10oz) canned chickpeas
  (garbanzos), drained and
  rinsed
1½ tsp ras-el-hanout
2 tbsp harissa
250ml (1 cup) vegetable stock
2–3 tbsp apricot jam (jelly)
  or marmalade
3 tbsp butter
Zest of 1 lemon
Sea salt and freshly ground
  black pepper

To serve
400g (2 cups) cooked
  couscous
1 tbsp chopped toasted
  pistachios
Small handful of coriander
  (cilantro) leaves
1 tbsp pomegranate seeds

1. Preheat the grill (broiler) to high.

2. Place the apricot halves, cut-side up, in a roasting pan with the cherry tomatoes. Drizzle with 2 tablespoons of the pomegranate molasses and season with salt and pepper. Place under the hot grill for 5–6 minutes, until everything is blistered and beginning to caramelise.

3. Meanwhile, place a flameproof casserole dish (Dutch oven) over a high heat and coat the bottom of the pan with a generous layer of olive oil. When hot, add the onion, fennel and carrots, season with salt and pepper, and stir well. Allow to cook on one side for 2–3 minutes, then stir to turn. After 2–3 minutes, add the garlic purée, chickpeas and ras-el-hanout. Stir to coat everything evenly and allow to cook for 30 seconds to toast the spices.

4. Stir in the harissa, vegetable stock and jam, cover with the lid and bring to the boil for 1–2 minutes. Remove the lid and simmer for 2–3 minutes, until the liquid has reduced by one-third and the vegetables are tender.

5. Remove from the heat and stir in the butter, lemon zest and the remaining pomegranate molasses.

6. Spoon the tagine over a bowl of warmed couscous and put the roasted apricots and tomatoes on top. Sprinkle with the pistachios, coriander leaves and pomegranate seeds before serving.

DESSERTS

American-style fluffy pancakes with flambéd pineapple

Americans sure do know a thing or two about making pancakes... They add baking powder to help them rise, or whipped egg whites to make them fluffy. For the lightest, fluffiest pancakes, I use both. As you can cook only one or two at a time, making a stack of pancakes will take longer than ten minutes. They are delicious for breakfast with bacon and maple syrup, but here I've made them into a dessert by caramelising some pineapple to go on top.

2 large eggs
2 tbsp sugar
180g (1½ cups) plain
   (all-purpose) flour
Pinch of salt
2 tsp baking powder
1½ tbsp vegetable oil,
   plus extra for frying
300ml (scant 1¼ cups)
   buttermilk or 280ml (1 cup
   + 2 tbsp) whole milk
1 tsp vanilla extract

**For the flambéd pineapple
(optional)**
2 tbsp caster sugar
2 tbsp butter
400g (14oz) fresh
   pineapple pieces
3½ tbsp rum

1. Separate the eggs into two bowls. Add the sugar to the egg whites and whip to soft peaks.

2. Add the flour, salt, baking powder, measured vegetable oil, buttermilk and vanilla extract to the yolks and beat together to form a smooth batter.

3. Gently fold the egg whites into the batter.

4. Place a small, non-stick frying pan (skillet) over a medium heat and add a little oil.

5. When hot, pour a ladleful of batter into the pan and cook for 2 minutes, until lightly browned. Flip the pancake and colour the other side, then transfer to a plate and keep warm. Repeat this step to make 7 more pancakes.

6. Meanwhile, cook the pineapple (if serving): place a non-stick frying pan over a medium–high heat and sprinkle in the sugar. When it turns golden brown, add the butter. When melted, add the pineapple pieces and cook for 3–4 minutes, turning occasionally, until caramelised.

7. Add the rum and carefully tilt the pan to ignite the alcohol. When the flames die down, pour the pineapple and caramel sauce over the top of the pancakes and serve.

**MAKES 16–18 COOKIES;
HOT CHOCOLATE
SERVES 2**

Ten-minute cookies with malted hot chocolate

Satisfy your cravings for freshly baked biscuits in just ten minutes! These are flavoured with cinnamon, but you could use ground ginger, vanilla extract, lemon zest or even a pinch of chilli, if you like. You don't have to make the hot chocolate, but I wouldn't want you to be twiddling your thumbs while the cookies are in the oven. The olive oil, milk chocolate and Horlicks make the drink wonderfully rich, but a cup of tea would be very nice too.

100g (scant ½ cup) soft butter,
   plus extra for greasing
50g (⅓ cup) light or dark
   brown sugar
⅓ tsp ground cinnamon
150g (1 cup + 2 tbsp)
   self-raising flour

For the malted hot chocolate
150ml (generous ½ cup)
   whole milk
1 tbsp olive oil
70g (2¾oz) milk chocolate
1 tbsp Horlicks drinking powder
Aerosol cream, for serving
   (optional)

1. Preheat the oven to 180°C/160°C fan/350°F/Gas 4. Grease a large baking tray (cookie sheet) with a little butter.

2. Put the measured butter into a bowl with the sugar and cinnamon and mix with a wooden spoon.

3. Add the flour and mix until thoroughly combined.

4. With clean hands, divide the dough into 12 equal pieces, roll them into balls and place on the prepared tray.

5. Flatten each ball a little with a fork, then bake for 7 minutes, until golden brown.

6. Meanwhile, make the hot chocolate: pour the milk into a small saucepan and add the olive oil. Place over a medium heat until warm.

7. Add the milk chocolate and Horlicks powder and stir to melt, then pour into a small blender or use a whisk to blend together for 2 minutes.

8. Pour into two mugs, top with the aerosol cream (if using) and serve with the freshly baked cookies.

SERVES 2

V

GF

Coconut stracciatella ice cream sundae

For this instant ice cream sundae, you need to have frozen the bananas and yoghurt in advance. At least four hours before serving, ideally more, peel and slice the bananas and put them into a bag, then pour the yoghurt into a clean ice-cube tray, and put both into the freezer. If you buy really dark chocolate for the scrolls, this dessert can be vegan.

4 bananas, sliced and frozen

60g (⅓ cup) frozen coconut yoghurt cubes

120ml (½ cup) coconut milk

2 tbsp maple syrup

Few drops of vanilla extract

1 tbsp cacao nibs

100g (4oz) bar of milk or dark chocolate

Pinch of sea salt (optional)

2 tbsp canned cherries, plus syrup for drizzling

2 tbsp toasted coconut flakes

1. Place two serving glasses in the freezer to chill.

2. Put the frozen bananas into the blender and add the frozen yoghurt cubes, coconut milk, maple syrup and vanilla extract. Blitz until smooth, then fold in the cacao nibs and place in the freezer in the blender jug.

3. Now make some chocolate scrolls: place the bar of chocolate on a board, shorter end nearest you, then drag a palette knife or flexible knife over the bar towards you, scraping the chocolate as you go.

4. Remove the glasses and blender jug from the freezer and use an ice-cream scoop to divide the frozen mixture between the frosted glasses. Top each one with a pinch of salt (if using) and some cherries, then drizzle over a little of the cherry syrup before finishing with the coconut flakes and the chocolate scrolls.

Blackberry and lemon Eton mess

Eton mess, the quintessentially British dessert, is both easy and quick, especially if you buy ready-made meringues. For this late-summer version, I've swapped the classic strawberries for blackberries, and grilled the meringue pieces to add that toasted marshmallow flavour. Folding shop-bought lemon curd through cream gives you a great accompaniment for fresh berries, scones or cake.

150g (1 cup) blackberries
2 limes
200ml (¾ cup) double (heavy) cream
100g (scant ⅓ cup) lemon curd
80g (3¼oz) ready-made meringues
Icing (powdered) sugar, for dusting

1. Preheat the grill (broiler) to high.

2. Put the blackberries into a bowl, add the zest and juice of one of the limes, then set aside.

3. Place the cream in a separate bowl and whisk to soft peaks. Gently fold in the lemon curd.

4. Crumble the meringues into pieces and put them on a baking tray. Place under the grill and watch until they just begin to colour. Remove straight away.

5. Fold the blackberries and some of the meringue pieces through the cream, then divide between four bowls.

6. Scatter the remaining bits of meringue over the cream, then zest the remaining lime over the top, reserving the flesh or juice for another day. Dust with icing sugar before serving.

Mango and saffron yoghurt pots with crystallised pistachios

I like to use Middle Eastern labneh in these delicious mango pots because, like Greek yoghurt, it has been strained, making it extra thick and creamy. Its gentle saltiness stands up to the sharp mango beautifully, and, when mixed with the cream cheese, will hold its shape without having to be put into the fridge to set. If you can't get hold of labneh, you could make your own (see below), or use thick Greek yoghurt instead.

Pinch of saffron threads
4 cardamom pods
3 tbsp honey
Zest of 1 orange
250g (1⅓ cups) shop-bought
   chopped mango
500ml (2 cups) labneh
   or Greek yoghurt
100g (scant ½ cup) cream
   cheese, at room
   temperature

For the crystallised
pistachios (optional)
60g (½ cup) shelled
   pistachios
1 tbsp sugar
Sea salt

To serve
Pomegranate seeds
Fresh mint leaves

1. Put the saffron, cardamom pods, honey, orange zest and 4 tablespoons water into a saucepan and place over a medium heat. Bring the mixture to the boil, discard the cardamom pods, then tip into the blender, add the mango and blitz to a smooth purée.

2. Meanwhile, crystallise the pistachios (if serving): place a non-stick frying pan (skillet) over a medium heat and add the pistachios, sugar and a pinch of salt. Gently toss or stir until the sugar has melted and coated the nuts, then pour onto a piece of baking paper or a silicone mat to cool.

3. Put the labneh or yoghurt and cream cheese into a bowl and mix until thoroughly combined.

4. Spoon some of the yoghurt mixture into four glasses or small bowls and add a layer of the mango purée. Repeat the layers until the glasses are full, finishing with a layer of the purée. Decorate with crystallised pistachios (if serving), pomegranate seeds and mint leaves.

IF YOU HAVE (A LOT) MORE TIME...
...make your own labneh: mix 500g (1lb 2oz)
Greek yoghurt with ½ tsp salt (optional) and
place on a clean square of muslin (cheesecloth)
set over a bowl. Tie the corners of the cloth
together, then suspend it above the bowl
to drain for about 12 hours. By that time, the
yoghurt will have the consistency of cream
cheese, but the longer you leave it, the thicker
it will be. Store the labneh, covered in the
fridge, for up to two weeks, and use in desserts
or as a dip, marinade or spread.

Fig and orange compote with sweet ricotta and fennel crackers

This fragrant pudding was inspired by baklava, the syrup-soaked pastry from Turkey and the Middle East. It's usually made with layer upon layer of filo pastry, and making it at home is very labour-intensive, but here I use just two layers of spring roll pastry, or feuille de brick to give it its proper name, which is easier to handle and quicker to cook. This recipe can easily be doubled or tripled to serve more people, but the time it takes to make will go up too.

1 tbsp plain (all-purpose) flour
2 sheets of spring roll (egg roll) pastry (about 25 x 25cm/ 10 x 10 inches)
1 tsp fennel seeds
1 tbsp brown sugar
1 egg yolk, beaten
120g (½ cup) fresh ricotta cheese
30g (1oz) icing (powdered) sugar, plus extra for dusting
2 figs
2 tbsp pistachios, roughly chopped (see tip)
2 tbsp walnuts, roughly chopped

For the orange blossom syrup
4 tbsp orange juice
2 cardamom pods
1 orange, a piece of peel removed with a speed peeler
2 tsp honey (see tip on page 108)
2 tsp orange flower water

1. Preheat the oven to 180°C/160°C fan/350°F/Gas 4.

2. Start by making the orange blossom syrup: put the orange juice into a small saucepan and add the cardamom pods and orange peel. Place over a medium heat and bring to the boil. Allow to bubble away until the liquid has reduced by half, then stir through the honey and orange flower water and remove from the heat.

3. Continue to peel the orange with a sharp knife, removing as much pith as possible, then cut the flesh into round slices. Drop the slices into the syrup.

4. Put the flour into a small bowl, add 2 tablespoons water and mix to a paste.

5. Lay a sheet of the pastry on a baking tray (cookie sheet) lined with greaseproof paper and brush all over with the flour paste. Sprinkle with the fennel seeds and brown sugar, then place the second sheet of pastry on top. Brush all over with the beaten egg yolk, then place in the oven and cook for 3 minutes, until crisp and golden brown.

6. Meanwhile, put the ricotta into a bowl, sprinkle over the icing sugar and mix thoroughly.

7. Cut the figs in half and put them into the syrup with the oranges. Stir to coat.

8. Spoon the ricotta onto plates and arrange the orange slices and figs on top.

9. Remove the pastry from the oven and break into large shards. Place a few shards on each plate, then sprinkle over the chopped nuts and a dusting of icing sugar before serving.

TIP FOR SPEED
To roughly chop nuts quickly, lay them on a chopping board in a single layer and lightly bash them with a heavy-based saucepan.

Rhubarb and marzipan tarts with orange mascarpone and toasted almonds

Spoiler alert – these tarts take longer than ten minutes to cook. I know that wasn't part of the deal, but they take only five minutes to prep, then 15 minutes in the oven, when you can be cracking on with the rest of the meal, so I hope you'll forgive me. The trick to the speedy prep is using ready-made marzipan, which gives the illusion of having rustled up a homemade frangipane but without any of the effort.

Butter, for greasing
1 x 320g (11½oz) sheet of
   ready-rolled puff pastry
40g (1½oz) block of frozen
   marzipan (see tip)
3 sticks of rhubarb
1 egg, beaten
2 tbsp soft brown sugar
2 tbsp flaked (sliced) or
   chopped almonds
120g (½ cup) mascarpone
   cheese
1 tbsp icing (powdered) sugar
Zest of 1 orange or clementine

CHEF'S TIP
Freezing the marzipan makes it much easier and quicker to grate. It can be grated into crumbles, mince pies or cakes for that distinct almond flavour.

1. Preheat the oven to 180°C/160°C fan/350°F/Gas 4. Butter a baking tray (cookie sheet) or line it with baking (parchment) paper.

2. Unroll the puff pastry sheet (following the packet instructions) and cut into quarters. Score a line around each piece 1cm (½ inch) from the edge and prick the surface inside the lines with a fork. Transfer to the prepared tray.

3. Finely grate the frozen marzipan evenly over the inside area of the pastry.

4. Cut the rhubarb into pieces as long as the marked rectangles, then lay them in neat rows on the pastry.

5. Brush the outer edges of the pastry with the beaten egg and sprinkle them with the brown sugar. Place in the oven for 15 minutes, until the rhubarb is cooked and the pastry has turned golden brown.

6. Put the almonds on a baking tray and toast in the oven for 3–4 minutes, until golden brown.

7. Meanwhile, put the mascarpone into a bowl with the icing sugar and half the orange zest and beat together.

8. Remove the tarts from the oven, sprinkle over the toasted almonds and remaining orange zest and serve with the sweetened mascarpone.

IF YOU HAVE MORE TIME...
...make a glaze by peeling the orange and putting the segments into a small saucepan with 2 tablespoons of honey. Place over a medium-high heat and bring to the boil. When the tarts come out of the oven, drizzle the sauce over the top.

Hazelnut tiramisu

You could make a really simple tiramisu in ten minutes, or you could push yourself to make this incredible chocolate and hazelnut version in the same amount of time... I know what I would do. The caramelised nuts and Nutella cream (other chocolate spreads are available) make it much more impressive and only a little bit more complicated to prepare. It can be served immediately, but could also be made in advance and kept in the fridge while you cook and eat dinner.

40g (generous ⅓ cup) hazelnuts, roughly chopped
2 tbsp caster (superfine) sugar
250g (1 cup + 1 tbsp) mascarpone cheese
3 tbsp Nutella
150ml (generous ½ cup) whipping cream
1 tbsp icing (powdered) sugar
1 tsp vanilla extract
8–10 sponge fingers
Cocoa powder, for dusting
Sea salt

For the soaking syrup
2 tbsp espresso coffee
1 tbsp honey
100ml (scant ½ cup) Marsala or coffee liqueur

1. Place a non-stick frying pan (skillet) over a high heat and add the hazelnuts. Season with a pinch of salt and toast for 2–3 minutes, tossing occasionally, until they are starting to colour.

2. Add the caster sugar and allow to caramelise, stirring continuously with a wooden spoon. Pour onto a plate or board and set aside to cool slightly.

3. Meanwhile, put the mascarpone and Nutella into a bowl and mix well.

4. Put the cream, icing sugar and vanilla extract into a food mixer or bowl and whisk until thick but not stiff.

5. Put the ingredients for the soaking syrup into a small bowl and mix together. Pour half into the Nutella mixture, then fold in the sweetened cream until just mixed for a ripple effect.

6. Dip half the sponge fingers in the remaining syrup, then place in the bottom of four glasses or bowls, tearing them to fit. Cover with a layer of the Nutella cream, then dip the remaining sponge fingers in the syrup and arrange them on top. Follow with another layer of the Nutella cream.

7. Break up the crystallised hazelnuts and sprinkle them on top of the puddings, then dust with cocoa powder before serving.

Mini cinnamon doughnuts with chilli chocolate dipping sauce

As these mini doughnuts are made without yeast, there is no waiting around for the dough to rise; instead, there's just ten minutes between you and an incredible homemade snack. Thanks to the ricotta, the doughnuts are golden and crunchy on the outside but light and pillowy inside, and amazing when dipped in chocolate sauce. You don't have to add the chilli, but it adds a warmth to the chocolate that really works.

Vegetable oil, for deep frying
250g (1 cup) ricotta cheese
2 eggs
60g (scant 3 tbsp) caster (superfine) sugar, plus 2–3 tbsp for dusting
125g (½ cup) plain (all-purpose) flour
2 tsp baking powder
Few drops of vanilla extract
1 tsp ground cinnamon
Zest of 1 orange

For the chilli chocolate dipping sauce
50g (2oz) dark chocolate
30g (¼ stick) butter
100ml (scant ½ cup) double (heavy) cream
100g (1 cup + 2 tsp) caster (superfine) sugar
2 tbsp honey
2 tsp chipotle paste
½ tsp sea salt

1. Pour a 6–8cm (2½–3½ inch) depth of vegetable oil into a wide saucepan and place over a medium–high heat until it reaches 180°C/350°F (see tip, page 168).

2. Put the ricotta into a food mixer or bowl and add the eggs, caster sugar, flour, baking powder and vanilla extract. Beat until everything is combined.

3. Using two clean tablespoons, form the dough into 8 walnut-sized balls.

4. Now make the dipping sauce: break the chocolate into small pieces and put into a small saucepan. Add the remaining sauce ingredients, then place over a low–medium heat and allow everything to melt, stirring regularly. Do not let it get too hot or the sauce will split.

5. When the oil is up to temperature, add half the dough balls to the pan and cook for 2–3 minutes, turning occasionally, until golden brown all over. Remove with a slotted spoon and drain on kitchen paper (paper towel). Cook the remaining balls in the same way.

6. Meanwhile, put the dusting sugar and cinnamon into a large bowl and mix together. Add the doughnuts and toss to coat.

7. Transfer them to a serving dish, grate over the orange zest and serve with the warm chocolate sauce.

Croissant French toast with butterscotch apples and sesame brittle

If you ever have any leftover croissants that need eating up – I'm aware how ridiculous that sounds, but just in case you ever do – you can't do better than make this dessert. Like traditional bread-and-butter pudding, it is even better with slightly stale croissants, so leave yours, if you can resist, and make this the following day. You could swap the apples for pears or peaches, depending on the season, and add a splash of apple brandy to the caramel for extra flavour.

4 croissants
120ml (½ cup) cold custard
2 eggs
100ml (scant ½ cup) whole milk
4 tbsp demerara (cane) sugar
1 large apple
2 tbsp honey
2 tbsp butter
Vegetable oil, for frying
2 Sesame Snaps
Icing (powdered) sugar,
   for dusting

To serve
Clotted or whipped double
   (heavy) cream
Pinch of ground cinnamon

CHEF'S TIP
Use a clean squeezy bottle to insert the custard into the croissants. It will make very light work of a fiddly job.

1. Using a knife, make a lengthways slit in each croissant, being careful not to cut right through them. Spoon or pipe the custard into the slits, then gently press the edges together to seal.

2. Crack the eggs into a wide bowl and mix with the milk. Submerge the croissants in the mixture, turning to ensure they are completely soaked.

3. Meanwhile, place a small, non-stick frying pan (skillet) over a medium heat and sprinkle in 2 tablespoons of the sugar.

4. Slice the apple into thin rings 1cm (½ inch) thick and place in the pan. Allow to bubble until golden brown and caramelised, then add the honey and butter and stir as they melt. Keep warm over the lowest possible heat until needed.

5. Place a large, non-stick frying pan over a medium–high heat and drizzle in a little oil. When it is hot, put the croissants into the pan and cook for 2 minutes on each side, until crisp and golden. Sprinkle with the remaining demerara sugar, then flip over and cook until the sugar has melted and caramelised.

6. Add 2 tablespoons water to the apples to loosen the sauce, then remove from the heat.

7. Put the croissants onto dessert plates and arrange the apples on top. Drizzle with the sauce, then sprinkle over the broken sesame snaps and a dusting of icing sugar. Serve with clotted or whipped cream dusted with a pinch of cinnamon.

Microwave sticky toffee pudding

Making a classic sticky toffee pudding from scratch isn't hard, but it does take a long time, so you wouldn't expect to find a recipe for one in this book, but I was determined to find a way. After much experimenting, these individual puddings were born. Cooked in the microwave in a matter of minutes, they are as sticky, gooey and deeply tasty as the real thing. You can double the quantities but, given that you have to cook each pudding on its own, it will take longer than ten minutes to cook more of them.

65g (scant ⅓ cup) butter,
   at room temperature,
   plus extra for greasing
2 tbsp chopped dates
1 tsp bicarbonate of soda
   (baking soda)
50g (⅓ cup) dark brown sugar
1 tbsp golden (corn) syrup
1 egg
65g (½ cup) self-raising flour
Crème fraîche (sour cream),
   to serve

For the toffee sauce
25g (scant 2 tbsp) butter
2 tbsp golden (corn) syrup
25g (scant 2 tbsp) dark
   brown sugar
60ml (¼ cup) double (heavy)
   cream

1. Butter a small microwaveable pudding basin.

2. Put the dates into another microwaveable bowl and mix with 3 tablespoons water.

3. Put the bowl into the microwave and cook on full power for 30 seconds.

4. Remove and mix in the bicarbonate of soda.

5. In a separate bowl, beat together the butter, brown sugar and golden syrup, then add the date mixture and stir thoroughly.

6. Crack in the egg, add the flour and beat well.

7. Pour into the prepared pudding basin and cover with a piece of kitchen paper (paper towel).

8. Place the basin in the microwave and cook on full power in 30-second bursts, taking the basin out each time and tapping it lightly on the work surface. Repeat 5–6 times, depending on the microwave, until the pudding has doubled in size. Allow to rest for 2 minutes.

9. Meanwhile, make the toffee sauce: put the butter, golden syrup, brown sugar and cream into a small saucepan and bring to the boil over a medium heat.

10. Invert the basin onto a serving plate and turn out the pudding. Pour over the hot sauce and serve with a dollop of crème fraîche on the side.

CHEF'S TIP
To help the cooked pudding absorb as much of the sauce as possible, poke the surface several times with a cocktail stick (toothpick). It will be even more moist and delicious.

Chocolate and honeycomb mousse

Fancy a rich and more-ish chocolate mousse that is ready in minutes? Look no further. This can be eaten, still warm, as soon as you pour it into the glass or bowl. Alternatively, put it in the fridge to set for a minimum of 20 minutes while you set about cooking the first part of your meal – ideal if you're entertaining. You can buy broken pieces of honeycomb (cinder toffee) in the baking aisle of most supermarkets, or make your own to take your mousse to the next level (see tip below).

350ml (1½ cups) whipping cream
2 tsp vanilla extract
200g (7oz) dark chocolate (60% cocoa solids)
1 tsp instant coffee granules
2 large egg yolks
80g (3¼oz) honeycomb (cinder toffee) pieces

1. Place a saucepan over a medium heat, add a little water and bring to a simmer.

2. Put the cream into a food mixer or bowl with the vanilla extract and whisk until it is thick but not stiff.

3. Break the chocolate into a microwaveable bowl and place in the microwave. Heat on the highest setting in 20-second bursts until melted.

4. Put the coffee granules and egg yolks into a heatproof bowl with 3 tablespoons boiling water and whisk to combine.

5. Place the bowl over the pan of simmering water and continue to whisk until the mixture has a custard-like consistency.

6. Whisk in the melted chocolate and the cream, then fold in the honeycomb pieces, reserving a few to decorate.

7. Pour the mixture into two chilled glasses and place in the fridge to set for 20–30 minutes. Sprinkle over the reserved honeycomb pieces before serving.

IF YOU HAVE MORE TIME...

...make your own honeycomb (cinder toffee). Line a baking tray with baking (parchment) paper and place in the freezer to chill. Put 90g (scant ½ cup) caster (superfine) sugar into a saucepan, add 1 heaped tablespoon soft brown sugar, 3 tablespoons golden (corn) syrup and 1 tablespoon honey and melt over a medium heat. Mix 2 teaspoons bicarbonate of soda (baking soda) with a pinch of salt and, when the sugar has reached a golden caramel colour, add it to the pan and mix together as it foams. Pour immediately into the chilled baking tray and allow to set before breaking into pieces.

Index

Acknowledgements

As I write this, in spring 2021, many of my restaurants across the world are closed. The coronavirus pandemic has affected virtually every industry around the globe, but probably none more so than the hospitality sector. I want to take this opportunity to say thank you to all of my staff for their perseverance and loyalty throughout this difficult time. We will get through this together.

I am so grateful to everyone who has worked on this book, mostly from the confines of their own homes, all in isolation, but pulling together to make the magic happen. The amazing team at Hodder have shown that no situation is too challenging... Thank you to Nicky Ross, Lauren Whelan, Isabel Gonzalez-Prendergast and Olivia Nightingall on the editorial front, and Al Oliver, Kate Brunt and Libby Earland from the design department. Thanks to Claudette Morris for producing yet another great book, Caitriona Horne for the marketing and Jenny Platt for the publicity. I am so lucky to be in such capable hands.

The *Ramsay in 10* food team has been incredible. A huge thank you to Jocky Petrie, Hayley Christopher, Amanda Berrill and especially Steve Pooley for all their hard work on the recipes. Thanks also to Camilla Stoddart for her bossiness and to Trish Burgess for her meticulousness – you make a great double act.

Shooting the pictures for a cookbook in lockdown was challenging to say the least, and I am so grateful to everyone involved for making it happen. A really big thank you to Jamie Orlando Smith for the photography, Jo Harris for the prop styling and Steve Pooley, again, for making the food look so amazing. Also, a big thumbs up to Nathan Burton for another beautiful design job.

Then there's the awesome production teams in the UK and US, who have filmed the *Ramsay in 10* YouTube series – thank you to James, Vlad and everyone involved at Whitecoat, and Micah, Kesha and the team in LA.

Thank you to the brilliant people who keep me on track every day, namely Rachel Ferguson and Katie Besozzi, and also a big thank you to Justin Mandel, without whom *Ramsay in 10* would never have come about.

Finally, a huge thank you to my lockdown production team in Cornwall, otherwise known as my daughters – Megan, Tilly and Holly. Thanks for all the camera work, the panning down on demand and the outrageous heckling. Seriously, girls, I couldn't have done it without you. Thanks to Oscar for all the background noise and general enthusiasm, and to Tana for her support throughout. And also thanks to my son, Jack, of whom I could not be more proud. You lot are the best.

First published in Great Britain in 2021 by Hodder & Stoughton
An Hachette UK company
First Grand Central Publishing Edition: October 2021

Grand Central Publishing is a division of Hachette Book Group, Inc. The Grand Central Publishing
name and logo is a trademark of Hachette Book Group, Inc. The publisher is not responsible for
websites (or their content) that are not owned by the publisher.
The Hachette Speakers Bureau provides a wide range of authors for speaking
events. To find out more, go to www.hachettespeakersbureau.com or call (866) 376-6591.

3

Library of Congress Cataloging-in-Publication Data has been applied for.

Hardback ISBN 978 1 5387 0781 4
eBook ISBN 978 1 5387 0782 1

Editorial Director: Nicky Ross
Project Editors: Lauren Whelan and Isabel Gonzalez-Prendergast
Editorial Assistant: Olivia Nightingall
Copyeditor: Patricia Burgess
Editor: Camilla Stoddart
Designer & Art Direction: Nathan Burton
Photography: Jamie Orlando-Smith
Food Stylist: Steve Pooley
Props Stylist: Jo Harris
Art Director: Alasdair Oliver
Production Manager: Claudette Morris

Color origination by Alta London
Printed in the United States of America

Grand Central Publishing
Hachette Book Group
1290 Avenue of the Americas, New York, NY 10104
grandcentralpublishing.com
twitter.com/grandcentralpub